"It's not everyday I come a
tifully written story, full of
a testament to the nobility
—Izzy Kalman, M.S.,
Buddies, Inc.

"The Cahill Factor is a story about courage and resilience, but it's mostly a story about love—not abstract or romantic sentiment, but the honest, gritty, feisty, and tenacious love that is the miracle of everyday life. Read it and be inspired!"
   —Eileen Kennedy-Moore, PhD, Psychologist and Author

"Everything about "THE CAHILL FACTOR" is a joy. Teena Cahill has a lot to teach us about living. What's truly remarkable is that so much knowledge is found in a book that is so easy and delightful to read."
   —Howard S. Mele, M.D. Formerly Clinical Director, The Carrier
     Clinic, Formerly Asst Clinical Professor of Psychiatry, UMDNJ

"With expertise, humor and grit, Dr. Cahill weaves the web of wisdom and resilience that provided support during a devastating event and gives readers the energy and insight to find their strengths and pursue their dreams."
   —Tamerra P. Moeller, Ph.D, Psychologist
   —James R. Moeller, Ph.D., Psychologist and Brain Researcher

"The Cahill Factor" is one of those rare books that touch both the mind and the soul. It is at once a tale of resilience and courage and a lesson in the ways that knowledge and awareness can illuminate the paths that each of us must find if we are to be both happy and wise. A must read for all who wants to learn the practical lessons which the new "science of well-being" has to offer."
   —Mark Glat, Psy.D., Psychologist

"Teena Cahill's book is full of wit and wisdom for all of us, both telling a great story and giving realistic and helpful advice on coping with today's increasingly complex world."
   —Robert Altman, Ph.D, President International Assessment Associates

"Here is Dr. Teena Cahill's love letter to all of us carrying a burden that feels bigger than we are. Her wisdom shows you how to bounce higher no matter how far or hard life drops you—with tactics that work in "the boardroom, the conference room, and the living room!"
   —Don Blohowiak, Executive Coach, Management Author, Lead Well
     Institute

"This is a truly remarkable story of the power of human connection and love. Poignant and well written, its message of hope is inspirational."
   —Phyllis Marganoff, Ed.D., Psychologist

"Dr. Cahill's awesome book delivers science through art, teaching lessons on living when presented with unexpected challenges."
   —Margaret Petry, Ph.D. Neuropsychologist

"The Cahill Factor is part love story and part life manifesto. Dr. Cahill talks about the marathon of life, but I read this gem of a book in a sprint. The humor, humility and honesty will open your resilient heart and fearless mind. She's a storyteller, a comedian and a powerful woman of the new millennium."
>   —Sasha M. Rash, President, Professional Beauty Association, TSA
>   President, Salon Sasha Inc.,

"Teena Cahill's account of how she tackled unexpected formidable life experiences with determination, wit and dignity is a model for seniors that may face modified retirement plans. A must read."
>   —Bernice Cassady, Chair, Edmonton Chapter, CARP, Canada's
>   Association for the 50Plus.

"Science has verified the importance of positive emotions for optimal healing and well-being. Dr. Cahill's book illustrates, with warmth, humor and authenticity, how positive expectations and hope can be mobilized to overcome adversity. This beautiful story touched my heart."
>   —Susan M. Stewart, RN, MA, CLL, Master Trainer, World Laughter
>   Tour, Inc

"This book is heart warming, touching and very intelligently written. I loved all the subjects it covered, as well as, the inspiring insight into human emotions and conditions. A must read for anyone dealing with the trials of caring for a disabled loved one."
>   —Erik Bayindirli, 2006 USA Paralympics Ski Team Member

"A warm, funny, inspiring and highly engrossing story of overcoming adversity, gaining wisdom and savoring the joy of life to the hilt."
>   —Grace Sinden, Retired Government Administrator and Conservationist

"Dr. Teena Cahill is resilience in person! Her book, "The Cahill Factor", captures her amazing story and grabs the reader for a phenomenal ride filled with humor, sorrow, and hope. It is a real-life love story and yet it is filled with practical advice. Tap into Teena's wisdom and experiences and find inspiration, admiration, and untapped reserves of your own capabilities to turn adversity into advantage!"
>   —Amanda D. Batson, Ph.D., Chief Executive Officer, ADB Partners
>   Education on Demand

"A true life love story that catapults one from life's harsh adversities to life's loving advantage and blessings."
>   —Mimi Warburton, Paralegal and Deaconess

"I enjoyed this book; I found it poignant and engaging, made all the more compelling because it is a true story. This is a story of love, perseverance, and personal initiative and is a wonderful example of the "don't ever give up" mantra, which the author and her husband have demonstrated in larger than life quantities, an example that many could, or perhaps, should, appreciate and follow."
>   —Robert A. Finch. Retired Airline Captain

The Cahill Factor

Turning
Adversity
into
Advantage

Teena Cahill, Psy.D.

SterlingHouse Publisher, Inc.   Pittsburgh, PA

The Cahill Factor

SterlingHouse Books

ISBN-10: 1-58501-110-X
ISBN-13: 978-1-58-501110-0
Trade Paperback
© Copyright 2007 Teena Cahill
All Rights Reserved
Library of Congress #2007923569

Requests for information should be addressed to:
SterlingHouse Publisher, Inc.
7436 Washington Avenue
Pittsburgh, PA 15218
info@sterlinghousepublisher.com
www.sterlinghousepublisher.com

SterlingHouse Books
is an imprint of SterlingHouse Publisher, Inc.

SterlingHouse Publisher, Inc.
is a company of CyntoMedia Corporation.

Cover Design: Brandon M. Bittner
Interior Design: Kathleen M. Gall
Photography by Image Arts Etc.
Images provided by iStockphoto.com

Printed in Canada

Dedication

To Brooks

*Had you not kept bugging me for the last decade,
this book would not have been written.
Without your courage, love, determination, and wisdom,
this book could not have been written.*

Acknowledgments

If we are really lucky, our children grow up to be the kind of people we admire and whose judgment we trust.

My daughter Mia and son-in-law Matt have encouraged me since I first began this project. Matt gave me hope when he read early drafts and pronounced the book meaningful. On difficult days, when all else failed, my kind and generous daughter sat with me at the computer and guided me through complicated passages. This book would not have been written if Mia and Matt, with whom Brooks and I live, had not been supportive in every way.

My son JC, a scientist with a critical eye, enthusiastically supported my efforts, then called me after he read an early draft and spoke from his heart about his emotional reaction to my words. Writing this book has forced me to put my feelings on the line, and if JC had not been so kind, I may have quit.

My son Andy and daughter-in-law Meaghan have been cheering me on since day one. Andy, after reading an earlier draft, called from vacation to tell me he would have liked the book even if his mother had not written it. His kindness and empowerment gave me the hope to go forward.

My stepchildren Matthew, Christy, and David, along with Matthew's wife, Tara, have each encouraged me to share with the world the lessons their father and I have learned. Christy is training to be a psychologist, and we have spent many hours discussing the events in this book and the concept of resilient living. This support has been invaluable.

David was still living at home when this story began, and his support both for his father and for this project have meant a lot to me. Matthew and Tara have also shared their enthusiasm with me at each step along the way, and I am grateful for their support.

Additional thanks to our kids for nine wonderful grandchildren, resilient souls in their own right, who add joy and meaning to everything.

My dear friend Jane comes from a family of writers, and her mission has been to give me overwhelming support, while at the same time trying to protect and caution me by pointing out the pitfalls of publishing. Jane's wise counsel gave me just enough protection to allow my leftover adolescent rebellion to rise up and drive my dreams forward.

This book is in your hands today because of the efforts of my good friends Kirby and Els, who led me to my brilliant literary agent, Rosalie Siegel. Rosalie began by confirming my kids' belief that the book had merit. She then spent countless hours working on my behalf. Rosalie is a wise woman and has been a great friend.

I have not met Dr. Aaron Beck or Dr. Martin Seligman, but their work in the fields of Cognitive Behavioral Therapy and Positive Psychology, respectively, has improved the lives of countless people, has given therapists solid strategies for treatment, and, because therapists are people too, has greatly influenced my own life.

Two years ago, while in Kentucky for a speaking engagement, I experienced a lucky twist of fate that led me to meet my editor, Susan Owens. Within minutes, we not only forged a formidable working relationship, but we also became new "lifelong" friends. I could not have finished this book without her hard work, good humor, and incredible editing skills.

Thanks to Karen Meltzer, my marketing manager, whose energy sometimes exceeds mine—not an easy task.

Thanks to the invaluable wise women—you know who you are—who have always been there to teach me what I needed to know. And I treasure the lessons taught to me by many supportive and kind men.

Then there is Brooks, whose power is so great that he is not afraid of mine. We remain deeply connected through our determination to go forward with hope, while at the same time continuing our passionate fights over politics and the best route to follow while traveling in the car. But that's another book.

Table of Contents

Foreword

"Action is the antidote to despair."
Joan Baez

I was 46 years old when my life changed in the blink of an eye and the flutter of a moment. My husband Brooks, to whom I had been married seven years and with whom I had merged children, homes, and busy careers, had a cerebral hemorrhage, a stroke, and later a spinal cord injury.

Before this event, Brooks, a former Marine Corps fighter pilot, was an international captain with a large commercial airline. I was a practicing therapist, adjunct professor, mother, stepmother, mother-in-law, stepdaughter, wife, former wife, and daughter-in-law. Like many women, I was sandwiched between aging parents and blossoming kids. I had just nursed my mother through the last stages of chronic obstructive pulmonary disease, my stepfather had recently had heart valve replacement surgery, and my mother-in-law was bedridden with congestive heart failure.

I had a busy practice and a great deal of professional

responsibility. Our six kids, ranging in age from late adolescence to early adulthood, brought with them both the chaos and the joy that kids bring in that stage when they have one foot in the home and the other in the future. They cycled in and out of our house, as they always had, and so did Brooks and I.

We were not the Brady Bunch, and there was no "Alice" to keep things running. A pet snake had been lost in the house for the last year; the dog had a hip problem; the ferret was becoming an expert at escaping from her cage, the last time making it into my bed; and the week before Brooks became ill, he had decided to put all of our financial records on his new computer. I didn't even know how to turn on his new toy, but I had bills to pay. I lived with all of the pressures of career and family that you live with and understand.

Then, the doctors gave my husband little chance to live.

Brooks' cerebral hemorrhage happened in the darkness of an ordinary morning just before Christmas. It was sudden, unexpected, and mind-numbing. Forty-five minutes later, as I followed the ambulance along slippery roads, surrounded by ice-laden trees sparkling in the moonlight, I had no way of knowing I was embarking on a life-changing journey, more complicated emotionally, and with greater possibility for learning, than any I had ever known.

I had always recognized the importance of resilience, courage, and leadership. These powerful allies kicked in as

I became a runner sprinting to the finish line, putting forth extraordinary effort to meet extraordinary challenges. Finally, he was no longer in imminent danger. The sprint was over. The marathon had begun.

This is my story. But it is also your story.

• • •

I am among the oldest of the baby boomers, born nine months after the end of World War II. In the 1970s, I was part of the mass march of women into the workplace—a workplace for which we were ready, but one that was not necessarily ready for us. I took advantage of new opportunities, earning a doctorate in psychology while, for many of those years, rearing my children as a single parent. Then I met and married Brooks, inheriting three stepchildren and a husband with a life as big as mine, who was not threatened by my ambition.

Thirty years later, I am still in the workplace, and sadly, most of the workplace is still not ready for women. Seventy percent of American families depend upon two incomes. Women make up more than half of those with two or three jobs, yet they still do most of the work in the home, are responsible for most of the child care, and are the first to be called when someone has a medical crisis.

At work, women may be punished financially or said not to be "team players" if they don't work late or take work home, or if they ask for benefits such as family leave, telecommuting, four-day work weeks, or flexible schedules—benefits that could make their lives easier, and, as research shows, the workplace more productive. Across America, women are responding to e-mails and working late into the night, long after the family is finally settled and asleep.

American women are competent, organized, hard-working, and dedicated workers. They take risks, understand how to manage people, keep their eyes on the bottom line, and have their backs up against the wall, fearful that one more responsibility will squeeze the very air from their lungs. If every woman in America walked out of the workforce tomorrow, this country would shut down. (We won't even mention what would happen if they walked out of their homes.)

Women care about work, but they also care about relationships. They have been nurturers and caregivers since the beginning of time. Most women I know could not live with themselves if they walked away from a sick spouse, an ill child, or a dying parent.

My daughter Mia, a former law professor and now a practicing attorney, has told me of research showing that, during divorce mediation, if the mediator is not aware of power-balancing between men and women, the women sometimes "do even worse," with respect to getting a fair settlement, than they would have in an actual courtroom. They trade away assets to preserve relationships.

Caring about relationships is a good choice, but I don't believe life needs to be a forced choice between taking care of others and taking care of ourselves. I also know that if we want our lives to change, we have to change them ourselves. No one else can do this for us.

The reality is, work affects home and home affects work, for men as well as for women. It is the demands and expectations—at work and at home—that are different. This is not fair, but then, life is not fair. Life can, however, be managed.

I refuse to be defined by life's events, pressures, or expectations, choosing instead to be defined by my reaction to them. Nature has helped us along in this area, because human beings are born **resilient**. This ability to bounce back from adversity, to handle life's problems, to juggle tasks and confront issues, is a magnificent connection that loops our minds and bodies into a single unit, forming an inherent "ligament" of support to carry us through tough times.

Nature has programmed this complicated feedback mechanism into our very being, a fact which even allows us to **benefit** from overcoming challenges. Responsibility and expectations force us to dig deeply until we find our **strengths**, use the potential within us, and eventually understand who we are and what we cherish in life—in other words, to find what psychologists call our authentic selves. This is what we are meant to do. After all, why would we be hard-wired to overcome adversity if we weren't expected to use it?

Our biological hard-wiring is a lifeline, one that

grounds us securely while at the same time giving us the flexibility to handle the problems life throws at us. Resilience is the platform on which we develop our strengths, find our authentic **leadership** style, and go forward into the future we demand. **We were born to lead**.

Do not tell me you are not a leader. It is not possible. What does a life not led look like, anyway? Your biology sent out the signal that started your mother into labor; you managed your way down the birth canal; you took your first breath and first steps. You have made it to where you are. The odds for success are on your side.

By the way, don't go looking for balance in your life. Scholars tell us exceptional performance requires focus and determination, and you will not perform well if you are suspended in midair like some overwhelmed cartoon character. Life events do not come at us in moderation; they come in twists and turns and towering waves, complete with unrealistic expectations. Balance is both a myth and a distraction. Life requires action.

I am not you and you are not me; the details of our lives are different. But when it comes to the basic principles of resilience, strength, and leadership, we are all wired in the same way.

I would like to tell you I was some kind of brilliant visionary, with a defined plan to follow, as I struggled to help save my husband's life and go forward with mine, but that was not the case. If it were, I could tell you exactly what to do in your situation: how to handle all of the responsibilities at work and at home while at the same time being true to yourself. I had no clear vision. Mostly, we get our vision retrospectively.

I don't have all the answers, but this I do know:

I trusted myself, even when others told me my goals were not possible. It's not that I didn't listen to or seek advice, but when push came to shove, I went with my strengths and my gut.

I took care of myself first, even when it appeared that I put the needs of others ahead of my own. There were times when I believed the needs of others were more important than mine, but at the same time, acting on that belief was a way of meeting my own needs, and benefiting me as well. If we look hard enough, we will see that even in our most altruistic moments, we are taking care of ourselves in some way. When you read this book and you think I am working solely in the best interests of others, look deeper.

I chose where to put my energy and my time. I didn't go around meeting the needs of others all the time. If others' needs or wants didn't fit into my sphere of responsibility, I did not allow myself to become distracted into putting their needs before mine.

I focused on my strengths. In each situation, I concentrated on what I could do and didn't worry about what I couldn't do. I went with my strengths. A resilient life is about getting up each morning, putting one foot in front of the other, doing what we think is right for ourselves and those around us, using all we have ever learned, and trying something. If it's not the right something—and often it's not—we take a deep breath and try again.

I refused to quit trying. Eventually, all of the trying and all of the "somethings" started to add up. One day I saw a faint path in the distance, a path lit with promise and possibility. However, it was only after I started down this path that I began to realize how often nature stacks the odds of success in our favor, how resilience really works. I was on a journey of growth, originating not from a defined plan I had made, but rather from deep within me, from my innate resilience. My strengths allowed me to continue the journey; my authenticity led the way.

Much later I realized that the end of the journey (if our journeys ever end) was more about feelings than about any specific goal. There are a lot of ways to flourish and be happy.

In the boardroom, the conference room, or the living room, both the sprint and the marathon require action. We are born tough, and we can enhance our resilience, find our strengths, and use our authentic leadership style to create the lives we want.

Life is not fair, nothing is forever, everything changes, we cannot control the world, balance only lasts in the moment, and it is all okay. I know this because I have lived it, and I have found a life far richer than I could have ever imagined.

Teena Long Cahill, Psy. D.

Introduction

"Turn your wounds into wisdom."
Oprah Winfrey

Rewind to the early 1980s

We met on a Thursday, the week after Easter, in a sleazy bar. (Brooks likes to describe the spot as a lovely meeting place of genteel folk, but the twinkle in his eye belies his most convincing explanations.) On that Thursday night I was a single parent, a full-time graduate student, and the mother of three kids. I was also an adjunct professor of psychology for a university that offered classes to the young airmen from our local Air Force base. I had a busy, fun, and interesting life. I was not looking for a new husband.

I had come to this watering hole, next to the Air Force base where I taught, against my better judgment. My friend Susan was meeting a date and didn't want to go alone. She persuaded me that I "owed her one," so I found a babysitter for the kids, put on a pretty dress (which still lives in a box under the basement stairs), and drove to this decrepit bar, the kind often seen around military bases. Within the first 10 minutes, I hated the entire atmosphere: I didn't want to drink; it was Thursday night and I had kids to get off to school the next morning and a class to teach. I didn't want to talk with anyone, either. In short, I wanted to go home. But my friend had disappeared.

Needing an anchor while I figured out what to do next, I took a seat at the bar. After a few minutes, as I alternated between trying to spot Susan's head above the crowd and thinking about bolting for the door, this compact, square-jawed athletic guy came up to me. He had salt-and-pepper hair, bright blue twinkling eyes, and a ready smile. "You don't seem to be very happy," he said.

At this point, all of my training, not to mention my interpersonal skills, deserted me. I looked at this pleasant man and said, "I don't belong here. I'm the psychology instructor."

Brooks laughed. His warm, kind face was embracing, and he felt somehow familiar. (A long time later, when I told him I thought he'd had a lot of "conventional suburbanite" in him, he remembered himself as something of a "cowboy," a "fighter jock," the last of a dying breed. As it turned out, he may have *seen* himself as a cowboy, but I knew how to use a lasso.)

Brooks explained that he was a former Marine Corps fighter pilot who now worked as a commercial airline pilot. Still a member of the Marine Corps Reserve, he was in town to command a squadron of fellow weekend fighter jocks for a two-week training session at the base.

Soon after we started talking, Brooks said goodbye to the folks he'd come with and suggested we meet for a drink at the nearby officers' club. Susan had found another ride home, and by this time a drink didn't seem like such a bad idea, so I agreed. Within minutes, we launched into conversations about politics, history, sports, and our dreams for our children. When we parted at the end of the evening, we both knew it was really a beginning, but I thought it unwise to get too wrapped up in him. After all, he was only in town for two weeks, and although our connection was exciting, it felt as if it could be a complication. My life was complicated enough.

The next day, the children and I were playing in a softball game at the university. To my surprise, Brooks found his way to the diamond. He suggested we go to dinner. Intuitively, wanting to keep our relationship on a level playing field, I suggested we play tennis. As we played, he did something that probably sealed our fate: He recognized my athletic ability and determination. Some women want men who offer fancy words, or roses, or diamonds. In my case, I like men who are not afraid of a woman's power.

I am a striver, setting goals for myself and helping others to set their own goals. When I meet people, I intuitively see their health and their strengths, focusing on what is right about them rather than what they think may be wrong. I try to empower people to find themselves, and when they can't, sometimes I carry them with me until they can. I like this about me, but I also know that I must take care of myself first, before I can be of use to anyone else.

Brooks, I soon learned, is a glider. When he comes in for a landing, if you don't get out of the way, he might run over you. Then, when the dust settles and you stand up quite disheveled, he captures you with his smile, his humor, and his intelligence. When I met him, he felt like a vacation.

We married a few years later, merging our complicated schedules to include the hours Brooks spent as a commercial pilot flying internationally, plus the hours I spent working as a psychotherapist. Season this mixture with six kids who cycled in and out of the house, add lots of time for travel, fun, and sports, and you get a taste of what daily life was like. Some called us a blended family, but as we grew together, we were more like a tossed salad, each person unique and true to himself or herself.

Despite all of its complexity, the salad continued to toss for seven years until the early hours of an ordinary December morning, when Brooks had a cerebral hemorrhage.

• • •

Fast forward to ten years after Brooks' injury

It was a December night once again, Christmas night, actually, and it had been a long day. Most of the kids (many now in their 30s), some accompanied by spouses and children, were home for the holiday. Presents and paper littered the living room floor, and the kids were going strong, talking, laughing, and catching up on each other's lives.

Although it was still early, I was ready to call it a night, and as I undressed in the darkness, listening to their muffled laughter, my heart filled with joy at their ability to have fun together and enjoy each other's company. Then I looked over at my sleeping husband and remembered the events of that other December, the one that had altered our lives so dramatically. It was always difficult to think about that time, and in spite of my delight in the kids' presence, I was feeling both restless and sad.

When we have an emotional reaction at the same time each year, and that reaction is in response to a past event that was traumatic or upsetting, psychologists call it an "anniversary response." I knew about this response; I had felt the same way in other Decembers. In fact, I almost had come to expect such feelings to fly out of some long-lost textbook and become a part of my holiday mood.

For a long time after Brooks' injury, the challenges of caring for him and dealing with all of the related changes in our lives had used up much of my "emotional space." I continued to have fun and was productive, but I had no room left for new adventures.

In the past few years, some of those challenges had become easier to manage. Brooks' cognitive abilities had continued to improve, and we had recently moved to a house more suited to our needs. Brooks had made great strides, and on that December night, I admitted to myself that it was time to make some strides of my own. As much as I wanted to stay in sync with him, Brooks was going in one direction, and I needed to go in another. How could I do this in a way so that we could still meet each other in the middle and feel connected? Brooks needed me, and I had learned by this time to understand, even with his changed abilities, how much I was enriched by his presence in my life.

This wasn't the first time I had entertained such thoughts, but that night something inside me began to shift. Perhaps it was the kids' laughter giving voice to my hope, to my need not to fail them or myself. Perhaps it was my natural resilience kicking in. I don't know, but on that night I started to focus on what I could do to bring new energy to my life.

For some time, images had been bubbling up in the back of my head. Now they were crystallizing into words: "I want to become a professional speaker and educator, sharing the insights I've gained over the past 40-some years. I want to talk to women about the expectations that are placed on them in the workplace and in their homes. I am trained through education and experience to deal with these issues, and I know there are millions of women out there who want to learn how to better take care of themselves. I want to empower these women, especially the younger ones, who often face challenges that the women of my generation—the 'liberated' ones—never dreamed of."

For most of my career I had studied the concepts of bouncing back from adversity, self-care, and using action to triumph over despair. In the years since Brooks' hemorrhage, I had lived them. I figured, given this combination of background and experience, if anyone could teach these skills, I could. It felt good to think about teaching again, but this time, it would be on my terms.

I was excited about this new direction and about the opportunity to help others, but I also realized I was embarking on this journey for myself. I knew that a part of my restlessness stemmed from the loss of my future, the future I'd put on hold to save and nurture my husband. Now I needed to find that future, *and* still be there for Brooks, *and* still allow him to be there for me.

As I recognized where I wanted to go, I began to plot what it would take to get me there. Soon I had a plan, and I smiled as I saw success in my mind's eye. Going forward with my plan would require that I stretch myself in new directions, learn new skills, and take new risks. This was my idea of a good time!

I felt charged with energy as I developed material, called an agent, and made tapes to show her how good I was. I bugged the agent for bookings and at the same time begged groups large and small to let me speak. When no one else would come, I packed the audience with supportive friends. After months of trial and error, one day I "hit my stride."

Since then, my life has taken a new direction, one that lets both Brooks and me remain integral parts of each other's lives, while at the same time allowing me to move into the future. It is a direction that has enriched us both.

I am not sad anymore. I am not overwhelmed, and

while I have always been happy, now I am happier. Life is tough, but because I've been able to use my resilience to tap into my strengths, I am tougher.

A few weeks ago I was pushing Brooks out of a restaurant in his wheelchair when two women, near enough to be overheard, looked at us with something between pity and disdain, then said to each other, "How sad... We are so lucky!" Brooks and I locked eyes, both worried about the other: he, that he was a burden to me, and I, that he might think he was a burden. Our concern for each other has always been the ironclad thread that binds us, and that evening we used it to forge a silent agreement within seconds. Concern turned to smiles as Brooks held tightly to his wheelchair. Urged on by the twinkle in his eye, "Grandma Teena" shifted into high gear. We raced past the startled women, laughing at our good fortune and determined to keep moving forward.

CHAPTER 1

Adversity

"When you're going through hell, keep going."
Winston Churchill

The field of Cognitive Behavioral Psychology teaches us....

- Choosing to change our thoughts is called a cognitive reframe.

- Our thoughts affect our feelings.

- Our feelings affect our behavior.

- I believe changing how we think can change our lives.

Brooks had his cerebral hemorrhage in the darkness of an early December morning, at a moment when it was least expected. I need to tell you this, because quite often life-changing events begin at the oddest times and totally without warning.

I knew immediately from his movement that something significant was happening, but I was unable to comprehend its meaning. Then Brooks sat up holding his head, screaming. The screaming gave way to loss of his bodily functions, followed by a hollow quiet. It felt like a scene from some terrifying horror movie. The feeling I remember most was fear. What I didn't feel, what I couldn't begin to absorb at the time, was that life as we had known it together was over.

Some moments are too surreal for us to process quickly, so in order to protect us, our natural resilience kicks in. We may go into "slow motion" as we distance ourselves from the world around us, struggle to figure out what is going on, and work to restore some predictability to the pictures we see. That's what I did after I called the police and waited, what seemed like an eternity, for help to arrive. I remember holding Brooks, then standing back and looking at him, just looking. We exchanged a few words, but I had no answers to his questions. Then the questions stopped.

In retrospect, I know I was trying to process the picture I saw in front of me. Brooks was dying. The silence and unreality of the situation were pierced when the volunteer emergency medical team burst through the front door, worked to stabilize Brooks, then carried him on a gurney out the back door.

This competent crew wasted no time, and within minutes I was taking an unplanned trip to an unknown destination. Every cell in my body wanted to turn the clock backward. Shock and hope were the only things that propelled me forward.

As I followed the ambulance to the hospital, I remembered the time, a couple of years before, when I'd raced over these very roads, with Brooks gasping for breath from a pulmonary embolism. I was comforted by the memory of flagging down a cop, asking him to lead me to the hospital, and hearing Brooks, ever the pilot, gasp to me in what was almost his last breath, "You're in the wrong gear!" (This time I knew where to find 5th gear, and I prayed that Brooks would shift into high gear, too.)

•   •   •

The week before had been miserably cold, and an ice storm had turned the roads into a scene from a Christmas card. Indeed, Christmas was right around the corner. I had put up the tree and still needed to finish cooking for the six kids who would soon descend upon us for the holidays.

Brooks was out of town that week, skiing with sons David and Andy at a week-long race camp in Park City, Utah. In prior years he'd been captain of his airline's ski team, and at age 55, still raced competitively. Now that the boys were in their teens, he looked forward to taking them out for race camp at the start of each season. Brooks loved to race, loved the kids, and really loved it if he could beat them down the powdery slopes, which he usually did. The kids were getting better, though, and this year David won.

The guys had a great time in Utah and were home only 24 hours before Brooks left for work on a trip to the Dominican Republic and Puerto Rico. When I picked him up at the airport upon his return, he looked gray and tired. Instead of going out to dinner as we'd planned, we went straight home.

The next day was Friday, and even though he grumbled about it, I insisted Brooks get a checkup. Later that morning the doctor called me, chuckling. He said that Brooks checked out fine and that I should think about a visit myself. There is nothing worse than a macho pilot and his doctor being forced to meet at the insistence of "the wife." This is a scenario ripe for ridicule, and I was irritated at the chuckles and the suggestion. *Very funny—ha, ha, ha,* I thought as I headed to my office.

That night, I arrived home ready for the weekend, in tune with Brooks and the season. In anticipation of a romantic evening, I put on a Johnny Mathis record of Christmas carols, poured myself a glass of wine, and settled in to catch up with the husband I'd hardly seen for the past two weeks. But Brooks was not himself. Normally a man of exceptionally good humor, he snapped at David and at me. At one point he even stormed out of the living room, saying he hated Christmas carols, hated Johnny Mathis even more, and wasn't too fond of me, either. I didn't know what to think.

Dinner was silent, and by the time we crawled into bed, I was fairly ticked off. I knew we were tired, but Brooks' behavior was both unusual and, I thought, uncalled for. *If he was that tired he should have gone to bed,* I thought. *No need for the dramatics!*

Before closing my eyes, I said my usual "I love you," but in a rather cold tone, a tone probably used from time to time in any marriage. From his side of the bed, Brooks mumbled something in return and fell immediately to sleep.

At about 2 a.m., I heard a noise and got out of bed to investigate. It turned out to be David coming home with two of his friends. The boys were on their way to our basement family room to watch TV, but I thought it was a little late, even for high school seniors. I suggested it was time to call it a night, and David left again to drive the boys to their house.

When I came back to bed, Brooks was filled with contrition and I with forgiveness. He was okay, and so was I. And then he was not okay, establishing in the blink of an eye a line that would forever separate our past from our future.

• • •

Although Brooks received top priority once we arrived at the emergency room, the wait between each procedure, each test, seemed interminable. Then the hurrying stopped. Eventually the radiologist came in and went over the CAT scans with me. The diagnosis: A vessel had opened in Brooks' head and blood was leaking into his brain. There was a lot of blood, but the scans could not pinpoint the exact source. Bleeding in the brain is not a good thing, and if you can't find where it's coming from, you're not likely to be able to stop it. For the first time, medical personnel began a mantra that I would hear again and again over the next several days: "He has little chance to live." The outer layers of my body believed this, and I called the children, most of whom were away at college or graduate school, to begin their sad journey home, but my heart and my gut would not accept the message.

By the next morning, Brooks exceeded the expectations of the naysayers and refused to die. He was moved from the emergency room to ICU, where sunlight peeked through the cracks of the green, heavy blinds that covered the windows of his cubicle. I felt grimy, the way you do after spending the night next to a hospital bed. By this time Brooks was quiet, not responding at all, and the room was quiet with him. Late that morning, a doctor visited and spelled out all of the possibilities, none of which ended with "…and your husband will be fine."

As I sat beside Brooks' bed, I was aware of the maze of medicine around me, of other cubicles of sorrow, of the stillness of crisis. Brooks was physically there, but emotionally I was alone. The strong, active man who was my husband lay motionless and removed from me.

Medical personnel came and went, performing those

procedures necessary when life hangs in the balance. When they were in the room I watched them, my eyes dull and my heart heavy. When they left, I returned to what I had taken on as my job, what I had to do to gain some control in this out-of-control situation: I sat next to Brooks' silent bed and I loved him, using my mind, my heart, and my voice to pour love and energy into this man. I leaned over his face and poured and poured. I needed to do something, and this was all I had.

This was **my** mantra: that his blood vessel would seal itself over, that he would hold on to life, and that I loved him.

Minutes became hours, and I noticed the sun was not peeking through the cracks in the blinds anymore. And then Brooks did an amazing thing. As he heard for probably the thousandth time, "I love you," he opened his eyes, emerging from the deepness of his sleep to say, "I love you, too. It's the damnedest thing…being tied to your feelings like this."

I looked at him and thought, *You are there! Somewhere deep inside that bloody brain, you are there!*

And then I heard a voice from deep within me. Perhaps it was the voice of my dreams, of my hope, of my unrealistic expectations. Perhaps it was the voice of Brooks' struggle to live, or the voice of my natural human resilience. Whatever it was, that voice we all choose to label with different names was there. I remember questioning whether it came from my heart or my head, but regardless, it spoke to me, and it said, "He will make it."

Despite the many voices telling me he would not, could not, make it, at that moment I made a conscious decision to believe *my* voice. Brooks had given strength to that voice, to my instincts, my hope, and my belief in his strength. We were a partnership, and he was telling me that both partners were still there.

I was afraid to touch him, lest I snap the thread on which he was balanced. So I stood up and walked to the window, surrounded by the bells and whistles of the ICU, and I felt power and hope pulse through my body. I wanted to soar, but during times of crisis, soaring is not my style. Instead I hunker down, get tough, and think. That night, I knew I would have to be tougher than I'd been ever before, and my muscles tensed with steely determination, as if preparing for war.

Former naval aviator and tough fighter pilot, the fellow everyone saw in Tom Cruise's "Top Gun," and a commercial pilot with decades of experience, Brooks had been a good instructor. And I had learned the lessons well. Following his instruction and my good sense, I thought to myself, *They told me 12 hours ago he was going to die, and he didn't. They told me 6 hours ago he was going to die, and he didn't. They told me 2 hours ago he was going to die, and he didn't. Here's what I'm going to do. I am going to plan on him living, and the moment he dies, I'll deal with it then.*

I was not in denial. I knew the risks, but I was choosing different thoughts, thoughts that led me from despair to hope, and ultimately, to action.

This is called a cognitive reframe. As a cognitive behaviorist, I know it was the healthiest thing I could have done for both of us, but at the time it was almost instinctual. At that moment of hope, I didn't give a label to this change in thinking, because it came as much from my gut as from my head. It's not that I didn't know Brooks might die: Everyone had been beating that into my head for hours. But he had given a voice to my hope that he would try to live, and I was going to listen to that voice, and to myself.

CHAPTER 2
Power

"None of us is as smart as all of us."
Blanchard and Peale

Experts who study how we organize our worlds tell us there are multiple models....

- The business world traditionally follows the pyramid model of organization: Success comes by climbing to the top and owning the most power.

- Another effective model involves weaving webs of connection that reach far beyond our grasp, forming networks of equals who support one another. I believe the tighter the web, the higher we bounce.

- Both styles generate power and are necessary for success at work or at home.

- It is important to learn how and when to use each style.

As morning turned into night and into morning again, the doctors tried to figure out what to do next, and Brooks tried to live. As part of their assessment plan, the medical staff would periodically conduct those tests familiar to all who have hung around neurology units. One such test checks to see if a patient is "Oriented Times Three"; in other words, does the person know who he is, where he is, and when it is—the date or the year. If he misses any one of these, it is not good. If he misses all three, it is very bad.

Even under those circumstances, it's a positive sign if the patient can respond. No matter what, responding is a good thing. Brooks was zero-for-three on the orientation test, but occasionally he would stir from his twilight life to respond. It was funny to hear his answers. This seasoned pilot, who had traveled the world, would be in Egypt, New York, Paris, seeing in his mind places he had been as well as those he had never visited. He was on a fantasy flight, but he was responding.

Good medicine, which is both art and science, sets in motion a treatment plan to give each patient the best chance for life, at the highest level of functioning. Observation—the ability to listen, watch, and become aware of patient responses—weighs heavily on the "art" side of the equation. When practiced well, observation can turn a good practitioner into a great one.

I am a trained observer. I am not perfect, and like anyone, if I'm not aware of myself, my own stuff can get in the way. However, I have a talent for picking up on what is different. For example, I usually can tell the minute I see a long-term client if something is "up." I don't know what's up (I'm not a mind reader), and I try not to make assumptions, but I am a good student of behavior.

I recall one occasion when my seatmate on a flight to New York was a young fellow who was clearly agitated, couldn't keep still, and was making everyone around him very nervous. My initial response, along with many of my fellow passengers, was to look upon this guy as suspect, perhaps even dangerous. However, in talking with him, I soon discovered that, rather than the terrorist we had feared, he was an athlete who had won a huge sporting event, couldn't reach his family before takeoff to give them the news, and was bursting with excitement. (Beware of assumptions! Behavior does not imply intent.)

And so, while I spent time speaking to Brooks, reading him the sports pages, hoping for a moment where we could connect, I also observed him. This wasn't a formal evaluation; it was more of a "wife" evaluation, although I was aware that my professional knowledge was interacting with my wifely intuition.

When I interacted with Brooks, I did so on a feeling level, as any wife would. At the same time, my experience as a clinician and as a teacher of psychophysiology helped me to trust the informal assessments my mind was making. I could sense changes in Brooks—his color, his movements, his smell—the tiniest things that only a partner would notice. These changes seemed vital to me.

Once Brooks said, "I can't hit the ball."

Rather than ask what he meant, I replied to this man, for whom baseball functioned as a life force, "But you must! You're the captain of the team. We need you!"

Brooks opened his eyes for a moment. Their normal blue turned cloudy gray, and, with a fatigued resignation that made me wonder how he got the words out, he whispered, "I'll try." (The fact that I actually would make Brooks the captain of the team is *still* met with great laughter in our family.)

Another time Brooks seemed to have constructed a prisoner-of-war delusion—not surprising, since I'm sure he must have felt like a prisoner. As I tried to orient him to where we lived, insisting that he listen to me, he roared, "You get in here! You get in here this minute!" He was ordering me into his delusion.

I thought of these events as progress, even milestones. I could see that deep down in Brooks' brain there was action, and I saw strength, determination, and resilience—all necessary components of possibility. (He may have had delusions, but the neurons were firing. When the neurons stop firing, we're toast!)

As the days went by, Brooks teetered between staying with us and leaving. He played imaginary games of baseball and football and went crazy with agitation when a nurse tuned in a basketball game on TV. He couldn't comprehend what he was seeing, and he had no short-term memory.

When the family walked into his room, sometimes he'd greet us with "Hi, great to see you!" (although if we left and came back a few minutes later, he didn't remember we'd been there and might say exactly the same thing). At other times he didn't seem to recognize anyone and appeared unaware of what was going on around him. No matter what his behavior, I always believed that he felt our presence. It was a handy belief.

Sometimes Brooks screamed in pain, and before he could be medicated, proceeded to pull all the tubes out of his arms. He fought the nurses' interventions. During one procedure—an angiogram to search for the source of his hemorrhage—he fought so hard that he overpowered the doctors and nurses, and they asked me to come into the surgical room to help calm him down. I must have felt familiar to him, because it worked.

Another message from Brooks, I thought, *another way to speak*. I told him I was listening. The results of the angiogram were disappointing: These new films still did not reveal the source of the bleeding. I saw this as a microscopic plumbing problem. No one could take action to fix the leak, because they couldn't find the leak. I poured over the films with the radiologist, hoping my untrained eye could find something that all of the trained eyes had missed. Of course, my efforts were equally fruitless, and we were left with nothing but questions. Would the vessel bleed again? Had it sealed itself off? No one knew.

I was told that Brooks might have a better chance of avoiding another hemorrhage if he were kept in a low state of arousal and not stimulated. At least that's what the research had shown, so it was decided to wait a couple of weeks before repeating the angiogram. I wanted more! I wanted action! I wanted to move Brooks to a university hospital, but recognizing such a move could kill him, I chose to wait.

In the meantime, Brooks was in a personal struggle with the forces of the universe. I couldn't relieve that struggle, but I was determined it would not be a lonely one. I prevailed upon friends, acquaintances, kids, Marine buddies, airline buddies, anyone I could find to make sure that Brooks was surrounded by love and support every hour of the day and night. I knew how important it was for him to constantly feel the presence of love. He had told me as much that first day, and I was listening to his plea.

For the first few nights I slept in the hospital waiting room, afraid that if I went home, I would somehow lose control, that he wouldn't feel me, that he would forget to hang on. Looking back, I am quite sure Brooks' life-or-death struggle had little to do with my physical presence, but at the time, my presence was all I had to offer, and I was trying to tip the scales toward life.

After awhile, Brooks' longtime buddy Jack spent the nighttime hours with him so I could go home and get some sleep. Jack is a character, well over six feet tall, with a bald head and a handlebar mustache. (I always think he looks like his picture should be on a box of cough drops.) He keeps up a constant stream of conversation, and his laugh is so powerful it can be recognized yards away. In fact, his buddies tell a story about the time Jack was on R & R during the Vietnam War, laughing at a movie in some Asian city, when a voice yelled in recognition from the back of the theater, "Hey, Jack, are you in here?"

Brooks loves Jack, and I knew he would hold on for him, too. After all, Brooks and Jack both operated from that hierarchical pyramid model. They had competed in the air, they had competed on the ski slopes, and here, too, I figured they would compete, each refusing to be the first to die. At least I hoped so.

Our six children, who at the time ranged in age from 17 to 25, quickly put their own lives on hold, trying to save us both. They remained with us, in various combinations, for the next several weeks. As I dealt with Brooks' life on an hour-by-hour basis, many others reached out to help support the fabric of our family's life. It took a lot of support to continue the struggle. I've always seen this outpouring as a testimony to Brooks, to the life he had lived and to the man he had become.

• • •

Brooks was born on a fall day, in a Midwestern state, to parents who were in their thirties by the time they married and started their family. His father, when told his first-born had arrived, held Brooks in his arms, walked to a nearby window, and remarked to his wife, "Look, dear. All those people down there on the sidewalk think it's just a regular day. They don't know yet what has happened."

Brooks was a smart little boy. His mom got him into a top private school, and his dad, with only an eighth-grade education but with a case of what I have come to respectfully call "terminal stubbornness," figured out how to pay for it. He figured out how to pay for Brooks' college education at Stanford, too.

After college, Brooks worked as a ski bum and taxi driver in Aspen, an occupational detour that made his folks less than happy. After a year of this, Brooks' dad arranged for a meeting with the Marines. Brooks was accepted, became a top naval aviator—think "An Officer and a Gentleman"—and flew fighter jets on active duty. After he left the service and became a commercial pilot, he still flew fighters as a reservist almost every weekend for the next twenty-some years.

Brooks loved his life as an airline pilot, and he loved the Marines, too. He had a lot of power, and his world included risk, danger, adventure, and many people who wanted to share it with him. He was kind to others, but mostly he was determined in his pursuit of what he wanted. At the time we met, what he wanted included me.

It was not an easy match. We are two strong-willed, determined individuals, and we both know how to get what we want. We have often said that, when we met, we each felt we'd discovered a part of something familiar in the other. I think it was trust.

I trusted Brooks in ways I never had trusted anyone, but I also set limits with this good-time fellow. His desire for fun and adventure was one of the things I loved most about him, but I knew from experience that the part of a person that most attracts us is also the part that will eventually drive us the craziest. So from the time we first met and understood each other so well, I playfully warned Brooks that he could do whatever he wanted, but he needed to be aware that whatever he did, I would do the same, times 10. My jesting-but-implied threat worked, and we had built a wonderful, committed life together. Now that life was under siege, and I was determined to fight for Brooks, for myself, and for our future, with all that I had.

At the time, in those long-ago days before ordinary folk communicated via cell phone and the Internet, word often traveled through telephone chains. In my case, once friends and neighbors heard what had happened, they kept track of my comings and goings and connected me with family and friends from around the world. And during the first days of this crisis, they put out the word to everyone they talked with: Pray for Brooks. Send out your vibes, your positive energy, whatever you call it in your life, but direct healing to this man. And people did.

A few days into the journey, the kids reminded me there was no food in the fridge, they were running out of money, and they'd been living on pizza for days. In response, friends and neighbors went into action. My former husband arrived from out of town to serve as chief cook and bottle washer, as did my lifelong friend, Carol. And for weeks, bags of food—delicious homemade and purchased items—found their way to our door, many from people I hardly knew, some from folks who never revealed their names. My colleagues in the mental health field also supported me by offering to take over my professional responsibilities whenever I needed them to.

This web of connection and love sustained us through each difficult hour, a web that stretched thousands of miles, into other countries, into the universe itself. I believe this web allowed me, in some intangible way I will never understand, to reach out to Brooks not only through my own energy, but through the energy of others. Their support empowered me, allowing me to do more than I ever could have done on my own. You might call this energy God or the power of love. I have no clue what to call it, and I know that those who sent it call it many things. Sometimes names don't matter. The feelings are the same.

While those outside the hospital walls were weaving their webs, inside the ICU a team of kids, friends, acquaintances, and colleagues was reaching in a single direction: toward Brooks. I asked everyone who sat by his bed to concentrate on him directly. I asked them to pray, to meditate, or to repeat their own mantra, instead of reading or being quiet. I viewed being with Brooks as a job, and I tried to get everyone who sat with him to work as hard as they could. Some people got mad at me. I understood, but I didn't care. I knew this was powerful medicine. Brooks had told me so. He was trying to hold on through feelings, and we were reaching out to grasp him with feelings of our own.

Everyone abided by my wishes, except Brooks' friend Jack. Quiet was not Jack's style, and he was uncontrollable, doing whatever he damn well pleased. He was loud, boisterous, and created a swirl of activity around himself. I vacillated between my worry that Jack would break that "low state of arousal" the doctors were promoting, thus perhaps stimulating another hemorrhage, and my belief that his spirited interactions were a different, equally potent kind of medicine.

In trying to give Brooks a chance for life, I was ever the teacher: giving instructions, sharing information, trying to apply anything that might be helpful. But I was also a student, and as such, I was learning valuable lessons for the marathon to come:

Never underestimate the strength of your webs.

Never underestimate the power of hope.

Hope—the belief that we can have a positive effect on the future—has been shown to change body chemistry in ways that move us to action. Hope is biological; we are hard-wired to benefit from the expectations of which it is made. When we feel hope, it inspires us, and I wanted Brooks to have that feeling. Some thought me bonkers, but on my mission to connect with him through feelings, hope was the conduit.

CHAPTER 3

Listening

*"It is the wise woman who hears one word
and understands two."*
Chinese proverb (with gender change)

**Many who study communication and leadership
suggest....**

• Leadership is about listening.

• In any conversation, it is the listener, not the
speaker, who is in charge.

• Leaders listen so they can form a vision for change.

• Managers implement change.

• Sometimes we are both leader and manager.

On Christmas night, after we'd been in the hospital for several days, Brooks started to go downhill. His awakenings were fewer and fewer. I couldn't feel him. He no longer tried to hit a home run or order me into his prisoner-of-war delusion.

I told everyone he was slipping away, but because I was not at the top of the pyramid of power, I didn't know how to make myself heard. In fact, I was getting lost in the pyramid, and if I couldn't find my way to the top, I feared Brooks could pay with his life.

December 26th was our wedding anniversary. I dressed up for the occasion, wearing the red, green, and white plaid slacks and white turtleneck that I wore every Christmas Day. At the time, I thought this costume might jog Brooks' memory, but in retrospect, I think I was the one who wanted to go back in time. Brooks probably hadn't noticed this outfit on the previous seven Christmases, and on this day he was noticing nothing. Only the radiologist, a kind man, told me I looked nice.

Two days later, Brooks began having multiple seizures that went on for hours and hours. Alone in my terror, I tried to communicate my fears, but it didn't feel as if my voice was effective. Was I just being seen as the anxious wife? I never denied that part, but I was an *aware* anxious wife. I was desperate. I believed Brooks was dying.

I had been working hard at weaving my web, and many, though not all, of the ICU nurses spent hours educating me. They explained that cerebral spinal fluid was trapped in Brooks' brain. Normally, this fluid circulates between the brain and the spinal cord, but because of the blood from the hemorrhage, the tubes that the fluid flows through to exit the brain were clogged. When the fluid can't escape, pressure builds up in the cranial cavity and the brain gets squashed up against the skull. Eventually, this pressure can do great harm; frequently, the patient suffers a stroke. When the pressure is intense, it can also cause seizures, and hours of uncontrolled seizures can have a negative effect on the brain.

This was why Brooks was not responding, why his level of consciousness, delusional as it had been, was going down. The pressure was building inside Brooks' brain as well as inside the ICU.

Despite the assistance of the nurses, Brooks was sliding downhill. Since nothing seemed to be changing the direction of the slide, I decided to take on the leadership role myself. With the pressure in Brooks' brain building, his blood pressure off the charts, and his body experiencing a running combo of seizures and vascular spasms, I called a neurosurgeon.

Although I admit that the wife is normally not the one to call for neurosurgery, I feared that not making the call could have resulted in Brooks' continued rapid decline and certain death. A nurse on duty at the ICU station refused to let me use the hospital phone to make the call. (Obviously, she was not in my web of connectedness and probably disapproved of my attempt to climb the pyramid. I often wonder if that nurse has ever been in a situation where following the rules could possibly mean the death of a loved one. I hope not.)

When I reached the doctor's office from a pay phone in the lobby, I asked that they get a message to him that we were in the hospital and that I wanted him to operate, to put a shunt in my husband's head that would bypass those clogged tubes and allow his cerebral spinal fluid to circulate. I told them I believed Brooks was dying and that I believed he did not have to die. The neurosurgeon arrived within the hour. It wasn't a moment too soon. Brooks was unresponsive. His eyes had rolled back in his head and he didn't even flinch when a nurse inserted an IV. In spite of all my vigilance, I feared I had waited too long.

Finally, though, I had "gotten it," and I was heading straight up that pyramid. It was a power grab to save my husband, and now that I had this skilled surgeon in my grasp, I needed him to hear Brooks' story. We went into a private room and I told him of my observations of the phantom baseball games, football games, and POW camp. I finished by telling him that the night before, Brooks had awakened for a moment and said, "There's a fuck-up, there's a fuck-up; call the lawyers."

The doctor looked at me with disbelief. After all, lying before him he saw a man near death. But it was true! Brooks was pleading for help, and whether he realized it or not, he *was* leading the team. He just needed someone to listen.

Because I knew Brooks was "speaking" to me, I was

listening. And when I spoke to the neurosurgeon, it was from both my heart and my head. As the listener, this doctor now held all the power. Fortunately, he listened well. He said he didn't know whether it would work, but he would try.

Within the hour, Brooks' beautiful gray hair was shaved and I watched him become a bald old man. It was the most beautiful sight I'd seen in days. I had reached the top of the pyramid and the pharaoh there knew how to listen. He also knew how to do neurosurgery.

Mia scurried to get Brooks' dental records so the tubes used in anesthesia wouldn't knock off any loose caps on his teeth. The rest of the kids arrived in stages: biological, step, and soon to be in-law. And a loyal Marine and his wife, a couple I barely knew and to whom I will be forever grateful, joined us as we waited the hours it took to see if Brooks' demise could be avoided, or if it was already too late.

Suddenly (though in reality hours later), the double swinging doors from the surgical suite opened wide and two nurses, each wearing one of those "shower caps" required in operating rooms, wheeled Brooks out on a gurney. Brooks wore a shower cap, too. He looked pretty silly, but he was *alert*! He was *laughing*! He was *slightly wild*! He was still delusional, still not oriented to time, person, or place, and he had no short-term memory, but he was interacting with us once again.

My joy was boundless. We were back to square one, paradoxically, a great achievement. Exceptional performance requires total awareness, focus, and concentration. The previous few days of beating down doors had been the exceptional performance of my life. Because the test did not show the source of Brooks' hemorrhage, I had chosen to go against my instincts, to not listen to my inner voice, and I had not explored moving him to a university hospital. My despair lifted when I saw Brooks come out of surgery, and for the first time in days, I did not feel desperate.

I felt as if I had been in a double bind, a no-win situation, and I was filled with the frustration and despair we all feel when trapped. Every cell in my body looked for a path to hope, and I'd finally found one in the neurosurgeon who led us back to the critical, but stable, situation Brooks had maintained during his first few days in the hospital.

Many hours later I had a meltdown, giving in at last to stress and fear. Once again my kids came to the rescue. I have a firm memory of Mia, my stepdaughter Christy, and my daughter-in-law Jen gently tucking me into bed. It was the most loving act I have ever felt. Mia and Jen have gone on to become great mothers, and Christy is on her way to becoming a great psychologist, but back then, for that night, I was their first child, their first client in crisis.

Their tenderness and the tenderness of my sons JC and Andy, my stepsons David and Matthew, and my future son-in-law Matt are etched in my memory. When I needed them, they were there, guiding me with their strength and wise counsel. They held Brooks' hand, watched him late into the night, did laundry, shopped, cooked, forced me to come home to shower, and made me drink apple juice. (I've never understood the apple juice thing!)

Later we discovered that Brooks had suffered a stroke. I wish all this had been avoided. Nevertheless, what happened is what happened, and we began to rebuild in this new reality.

CHAPTER 4

Decisions

---

*"The game of life is
not so much in holding a good hand,
as in playing a poor hand well."*
H. T. Leslie

- There are times when there is no right or wrong decision.

- Often we calculate our risks, make a decision, and work to make it right.

- Good decision-making means we "give it our best shot," using all we know. Sometimes it means we learn from our mistakes and decide again.

The day after the neurosurgeon installed the shunt in Brooks' head, I arrived at his bedside to find a staff member performing a neurological test. It was one of those tests where the practitioner moves a finger in front of the patient's eyes to see if he can follow, and how far to each side he can see. As I watched this test, I saw that Brooks had no peripheral vision in his right eye. That's when I first knew that he'd had a stroke.

Our general understanding is that the left side of the brain controls the right side of the body, and the right side of the brain controls the left side of the body. But the eyes are a little different. Because nature wants to protect our eyesight, both sides of the brain affect our vision in each eye. That way, should we have a serious head injury, we have a greater chance of retaining some of our vision—one more example of how we are built for survival. Brooks' stroke was in the right side of his brain, and he had lost his vision on the extreme right side of his right eye.

I wasn't happy about his stroke, but I was relieved that we had been able to restore him to a more stable level. He had a slight fever, however, and not wanting another complication to impede his progress, I was hyper-vigilant, almost waiting for "the other shoe to drop," and hoping against hope that it wouldn't.

Although patients can sometimes develop what is called a post-operative fever, which is normally not a cause for alarm, I didn't believe Brooks' fever fell into this category, and I was right. As I continued to observe him, he became less and less communicative. By the evening of the second day, the dull gray eyes were back, and then they closed. As he drifted in and out of consciousness, his temperature soared. Once again, he was critically ill.

I wasn't going to make the same mistake twice, so I demanded tests. They X-rayed his lungs, looking for pneumonia. They tested his heart. They prodded his stomach. When we discovered a red line leading up his arm from an old IV site, we finally had the answer.

Hospitals can be dangerous places, and germs like staphylococcus are rampant. There are many procedures in place to help prevent the spread of these dangerous opportunists, but death from a hospital staph infection is still all too common. I was livid. I had been working without rest to save him, but these germs, these invisible microscopic death machines, had been working too. This wasn't a shoe dropping. This was a kick in the gut by a combat boot.

Brooks seemed to be dying once again. Because he was unable to comprehend anything and flailing wildly in his fight to survive, his hands had to be tied to the bed rails. Two of the children and I took shifts sitting with him. We were all exhausted.

When JC or I sat with him, Brooks was well behaved. As soon as he was left alone with Christy, he succeeded in freeing his hands by quietly working at the gauze knots that secured his wrists. I saw this as a sign of hope. Again, deep in his brain, below where he showed any recognition of us, Brooks had some level of awareness and was making judgments. I didn't think it was accidental that he chose to try to escape on Christy's watch. He thought, incorrectly, that he could intimidate her because she was a girl. Boy, was I going to be mad at him when this was over. And this *needed* to be over, soon.

Almost since he was first admitted, I had wanted to move Brooks to a university hospital, but because the angiogram had not located the source of the bleeding, I was afraid to do this; instead, I chose to wait until the doctors could repeat the procedure. Now, because of his fever, they couldn't perform the test, since doing so could spread the infection throughout his body. I felt stuck, in a double bind, and if I were stuck, so was Brooks. I also knew, however, that taking no action was in fact an action. It was time to make a decision one way or the other.

I started some serious weaving, spending the next few days calling every physician I knew and asking what they would do in the same situation. We needed as much information as we could get, and I wanted to make certain that the route I chose was the right thing for Brooks, not just a reaction to my increasing anxiety. This decision had to be in Brooks' best interest. But it was not for Brooks alone.

• • •

Brooks is the oldest of three boys. His parents, who were then 87 and 88, had moved several years earlier from the Midwest to breezy Florida. Their funky little incorporation of mobile homes sits near the ocean, occupying some of the most expensive real estate in North America. Developers have been trying to get that land for years, but paradise is not for sale.

Some of the mobile homes are large and spacious, but Brooks' parents had a modest, economy model. No doubt about it, it was a trailer. The little haven they called home was also sometimes called "The Tuna Can" by yours truly, their obnoxious daughter-in-law. (I still feel guilty about this designation.)

Despite my snide remarks, however, I dearly loved my mother-in-law. She was a beautiful, intelligent, and funny woman, unfailing in her kindness to me and my children. Most importantly, she was a loving and kind mother to her boys. And she was dying. She and Brooks' dad had retired to Florida after her heart attack years earlier, and she was now in the last stages of congestive heart failure. There had been many emergency hospitalizations during the previous year, each nearly ending in her death.

"Brookie" was the apple of his mother's eye. Over the years, she had felt both terror and pride in his exploits as a military fighter pilot and later as a civilian airline captain. She was proud of her boy, and she loved to sit with him on the sofa, looking at old pictures from his childhood.

Of course, his mom didn't know everything about her oldest son. Once, during Brooks' teen years, she opened the mailbox to find that pornography had been delivered to their home. She was outraged that such unsolicited material would arrive on her doorstop and later traveled with a friend to testify before some government committee that was investigating the pornography industry. Whenever she told the story of how she had fought back against this vile invasion on behalf of the American family, Brooks smiled and hugged his mother with pride. Only later did he confess to me, chastened and red-faced, that it was he, the beloved son, who had ordered the porn.

At first, Brooks' mom and I bonded because we both loved Brooks, but in time we became close because we loved each other. I delighted in giving her gifts and taking her flowers. She was always appreciative and made me feel as if I were the most intelligent person in the world to have found these special gifts for her. She called me her "angel" and I basked in her warmth.

When I called Brooks' folks on that bleak December night to tell them the news of his hemorrhage, I felt their pain through the phone wires. It killed me to tell them. As a wife, I thought of Brooks, but as a mother, I thought of sons, daughters, stepchildren, in-laws. *Please, God,* I thought, *let me never get this call.*

But Brooks' folks did get the call, and I was the one who had to place it. Later, I asked others to keep them in the daily loop, and I called them personally every few days. I set up this arrangement, I told them, because I was so focused on Brooks, and they said they understood, but it was a lie. I had others call because it broke my heart to tell them the truth. I didn't want them to know what I knew. I didn't want them to feel what I felt. I couldn't tell them their son might die, because I didn't want to acknowledge that it might be true.

As I continued to wrestle with the decision that had no certain answer, I felt the presence of all the people whose lives would be affected by my choice. I thought about Brooks' parents; I thought about the children, both his and mine. I was the sentry standing watch over his life, and those that loved him the most had to trust me. They had no option but to trust me, so I had to do it right for all of us. Finally, I made the decision to move Brooks to a university hospital.

Through my good friend Jane and Brooks' buddy Bob, my web eventually reached the chief of neurosurgery at a major university hospital in a nearby state. This famous man listened as I poured out my story over the phone. In fact, not only did he listen, he advised, and he agreed with my instincts to go ahead with the move. And then he said the most wonderful words I had heard in weeks: "I'll have my assistant call and tell them we're on our way. Sign him out. I'm sending a helicopter."

Yes! Yes! Yes!

I ran back to Brooks' room to tell him he was going on a helicopter ride, but he didn't understand. However, when Christy and I watched him being loaded lovingly onto the chopper, we could not miss the smile on his face that went from ear to ear.

I had made an informed decision and I felt a heavy weight lifted from my shoulders. It was then that I called

Brooks' parents. By this time, both were weak and weary, especially his mom. She could barely talk, but I was joyful. So I made her a deal. "Promise me you will hang on! As soon as the doctors allow it, I promise that I will bring Brooks to see you." I asked her to wait for us, and she agreed.

When Brooks was released from the hospital, his mom was still hanging on, but there was little time left. The doctors said flying was out of the question, so with both Brooks and his mom in my heart, and a healthy dose of mother's love, I drove him to Florida, covering the hundreds of miles between our homes with only a one-night stop.

We arrived exhausted, but we arrived in time. Almost two months to the day after I'd asked her to wait for us, Brooks and I pulled up to the door of "The Tuna Can," and I delivered this beloved son into the arms of his mother.

I sobbed, Brooks' dad sobbed, and Brooks sobbed. His mom, both weary and determined, reached up from her hospital bed, which had been put in the sitting area next to the kitchen, wrapped her heavy, weak arms around her firstborn son, and held him like there was no tomorrow.

And there wasn't. The next day she entered the hospital, went from there to hospice, and then on to the one she called her heavenly father, who had allowed her to hold her son one last time.

CHAPTER 5
Hope

---

*"Hope is the thing with feathers that perches in the soul,
and sings the tune without the words
and never stops at all."*
Emily Dickinson

Neurobiologists who study how our thoughts affect us physically have found....

- Human beings are hard-wired to benefit from the belief that they can have a positive effect on their future. This phenomenon is called hope.

- Biological reactions in our brain that accompany the feeling of hope can help us to change how we look at things.

- As our perceptions change, so do our actions.

- I believe hope is the road that takes us from fear to courage.

But let's not get ahead of the story. When Brooks was carried off the chopper at the university hospital, JC was waiting, and Christy and I arrived moments later. Responding to Brooks' complaint of a headache, doctors first performed an emergency angiogram and then moved him to ICU on the state-of-the-art neurology floor. His bed was surrounded by glass so that he could be observed from every position in the unit, and his hands were free of restraint. The "torture" of his hands being tied to the bed rails was over, and my pain began to lessen too.

Unfortunately, the new angiogram didn't reveal the source of the bleeding either, so the only thing to do was to assess the amount of damage done by the hemorrhage and to deal with the problems Brooks had developed in the meantime.

One of these problems was that Brooks had lost a great deal of weight. He couldn't eat without severe pain, and even sips of liquid resulted in terrible screaming, but he couldn't say what was wrong. The medical staff quickly discovered the problem: Reflux from all of the medications he'd been given had caused severe burns in his esophagus.

In spite of my relief, I knew these doctors, skilled as they were, didn't have all the answers. I also knew that no one could predict the future, but, even so, I felt safe enough to let down my guard and begin to breathe once again. Sometimes I even caught myself laughing. I was conscious of walking through the hospital with a strange lightness in my arms and legs, the kind you have when you realize that you've backed away from a cliff and tragedy does not await your next step.

One afternoon I watched as the ICU nurses tried to stimulate Brooks into responding so they could assess his cognitive potential. They seemed to get his attention when they started talking about Elvis Presley, who had been in the news that week. (Professionals that they were, they had figured out they had an old "frat boy" from the '50s on their hands.)

Brooks has an amazing knowledge of music legends, especially in jazz and rock and roll (acquired, I'm sorry to say, from drinking beer in jazz clubs during his teen years). He knew many of the famous country and western singers, folk singers, and rockers before they were legends, and his stories had always been great fun.

In bed that night, I fantasized that maybe those nurses had been able to get Brooks to talk. Maybe they'd heard all about how he used to count the money in the back room after performances by fledgling artists like Johnny Cash. After all, since his long-term memory was not impaired, he'd probably regaled them with his knowledge.

The next morning I learned that, although he had laughed at the nurses' stories, he'd had no comment at all. Brooks was beginning to look like he always had: His thick mop of wavy gray hair was starting to grow back, and the color was returning to his cheeks, but although he was "better," he wasn't Brooks.

For the past few weeks, although I knew intellectually

that he had suffered brain damage, I'd been so focused on keeping him alive that I hadn't let myself think about how that brain damage would translate into daily life. That morning I began to acknowledge the deep chasm between survival and "the way things used to be." What if he never got better? For the first of many times along the road to come, I asked myself that question, and for the first of many times, I began to adjust my expectations to the reality of what "better" might mean.

• • •

Several days later, and for the first time since our saga began, Brooks improved enough to get a promotion. It was a happy day when he was moved to an observation room, still all glass and still in front of the nurses' station, but on the regular neurological floor, out of the ICU. Hope poured from my heart.

I've always told my kids that feelings are like green slime. If you don't let them out, they ooze from your pores and you get all slippery, unable to get close to anyone. For the last several weeks, I had closed myself off, put my head down, and done what I thought I needed to do. As a result, I'm sure a lot of feelings oozed from my pores, and I knew some people resented my total preoccupation with moving Brooks to a university hospital. Now I felt safe enough to let some of those feelings out—not just my anxious feelings, but my hopeful ones, too. I was beginning to feel like myself again, and when I lifted my head, I noticed the sun.

Brooks progressed to the point of watching TV. He was still not oriented times three, but he did enjoy a football game and really enjoyed seeing a commercial about a juicy hamburger. Although the word "hamburger" escaped him, he pointed at the TV, shouting, "I want one of those! I want one of those!" When his esophagus had healed to the point that the doctors determined he could eat solid food, a nurse who'd been in the room that day arranged for him to have a hamburger. Medicine and humanity, what a tonic.

From the day of our arrival at University Hospital, everyone treated Brooks and me with dignity and as part of the team. As they dealt with his problems, I began to think that, not only might Brooks live, but he also might have a future. I hadn't thought much recently about the future; it had been enough to make sure we made it from moment to moment. Now I dared to have a goal. I wanted to take Brooks home.

I won't suggest that this hospital didn't mess up now and again; we all do. Patients need an advocate looking out for them, no question. But when I stopped a resident from giving Brooks a medication I knew he couldn't tolerate due to an allergy, the chief of neurosurgery came to thank me. It doesn't get any better than this, because everything—in medicine, in business, in our personal lives—is about relationships, and relationships are based on communication and respect.

Medicine is an inexact science and subject to human error, so mistakes happen, but the people in this hospital were great communicators. In this imperfect but balanced harmony, Brooks began to heal. Days became weeks, and eventually he was ready to go home.

He still couldn't retain the knowledge of where he was: The best he could remember was that he was in a big hospital in the Midwest. Not quite right, but not Egypt, either. He also had no idea of the relationship between one place and another. One day, when he had a stuffy nose, he saw a commercial for a humidifier on TV and remembered he had seen one in a ski condo in Utah. He asked me to go and pick it up, assuming I could be back before the commercial was over. At least he remembered there was a Utah. I saw promise!

Brooks also remembered he was a pilot. One day he asked me when he could go back to work. My heart broke with that question, because along with skiing, flying was Brooks' true passion.

In fact, one of our running jokes went this way. He would tell me he loved me, and I would quiz him, "Do you love me as much as tennis?"

"Yes."

"Do you love me as much as football?"

"Yes."

Then I'd ask if he loved me as much as skiing or flying. Brooks' eyes would get that familiar twinkle, and he would start hedging. "Hmm, hmm." Finally, with his face drawn up as if he were pondering a very difficult question, he would teasingly answer, "Of course, dear," and we would both convulse with laughter.

So when he asked me about flying, I fudged. Scientists tell us that hope can have a positive biological effect on our brains, and Brooks needed all the hope he could get. Time would teach him new realities, and new realities might bring hope renewed.

When it was time for Brooks to be released, the doctor called me into his office and said, candidly, "I don't know what you have here, Teena. He might be a vegetable." This doctor was a nice guy, and we had come to respect each other. I appreciated his honesty, but I didn't agree. I knew Brooks was not going to be a vegetable. He had remembered he was a pilot; he had remembered Utah.

I was probably escaping into my fantasy of normalcy again, but it wasn't an actual choice. My joy at Brooks' escape from death, and the physical lightness and relief that accompanied that joy, were propelling me forward step-by-step, day-by-day. On this day, I was stepping out of the hospital with a man whom many had believed would never take a step again. I was not about to let someone else's uncertainty trip us up, and at that point I was too tired to think anyway. I wanted to go home, and I wanted to take Brooks with me. No matter what happened next, he was alive, and this alone was a great victory.

CHAPTER 6
Courage

"Courage is just fear held one moment longer."
General George S. Patton, Jr.

- Courage is not just for the soldier on the battlefield.

- Sometimes it takes courage just to get up in the morning.

- But courage is contagious: When you see it all around you, you are forced to grow past your fear.

Once Brooks began to improve, I learned to adapt to the university hospital environment and to Brooks' reactions within that environment. When he behaved like a patient on a neurological floor, when he acted like a guy who had suffered a stroke and had memory loss, it seemed normal for the situation. When he told me to run off to Utah to get the humidifier during that TV commercial, it was sweet. When he failed to be oriented to place or time, it seemed appropriate. And when he had no memory of the events of the day before each new day, I understood why. I had accepted this definition of "better," and as long as we were in a hospital setting, it made sense.

What I hadn't understood were my unexamined expectations about Brooks' behavior once we returned to "normal" life. As it turned out, I had a lot to learn, and my education began on the way home from the hospital. We were in my little four-seat coupe, a fun-loving machine Brooks had found for me five years before, after my old car had died. It had been many long weeks since the ambulance had come to our now-deserted home and whisked Brooks, the life he knew, and the lives we had taken for granted, so very far away. Now, we were taking a victory lap. We had won.

The Brooks sitting next to me, however, was not the healthy, robust fellow he'd been before his injury. In fact, his neck hurt so much that he couldn't hold his head up. This was the first sign, we learned a couple of years later, of a spinal cord injury that, combined with his other problems, would limit his ability to walk for the rest of his life. On that day, though, the future was unknown and far away, and my little car scooted up the road toward home, me happily at the wheel, Brooks resting his head on a pillow.

I first realized something more than his sore neck was different when Brooks demanded I take a bizarre alternate route to get home. A fight ensued. He was insisting I go miles and miles out of the way, apparently forgetting the route that we had both driven hundreds of times before. He would not give in, and, weary from bombarding him with rationality, I went his way.

Today we laugh about his alternate routes, like the time he insisted we take a shortcut from Colorado to Nebraska by going through Wyoming! This 6-hour trip became 11, and in years to come, I learned to give in to his new geographical realities when I had time and it didn't matter, and to hold my ground when it did. It's telling the difference between the two that is the problem, but on that sunny day, I had yet to master that lesson.

By the time we left the university hospital, we had exhausted our friends and family. The kids all needed to go back to work or school, and the hospital was many miles from where we lived. In the last few weeks it had been pretty much Brooks and me, with the exception of JC and his wife, who were living nearby. Everyone had put aside their own needs to help us, but I could feel, by the lessening of phone calls and visits, that they were exhausted by the experience. These are normal responses, and although

I knew in an emergency I could call for help and people would still be there for us, there comes a time in life when we need to make things work for ourselves.

And so we arrived home to an empty house, and when we first walked in the door, it felt as if time had stopped. The skeleton of the Christmas tree, its sharp dried needles littering the floor, stood as a lonely sentinel in the living room window. The bed was crumpled and unmade, the refrigerator bare, and a brief power outage days before had left every clock in the house blinking some kind of reminder...or was it a warning?

Amidst this chaos, Brooks stood in our sunny kitchen, his blue eyes finally free of their gunmetal dullness, and began to tell me a story. It was a good story, delivered by a man who always had a lot of authority. The problem was, it wasn't a true story. In that moment I saw his brain damage in a new and startling way.

It was as if there were three little "word balloons" (like the ones in comic strips) floating above his head. Each balloon held a story, but each story was different and unrelated. In my mind's eye, I saw him reach his hand into the first balloon for the words to begin, into the second for more detail, and then into the third balloon, where he found a suitable ending.

Psychologists call this "confabulation," an organic problem that I had studied in classrooms and observed in clinical situations. In that moment, however, Brooks taught me more about neuropsychological assessments than I ever had learned in the classroom, in a hospital, or through an internship. No longer was the problem confined to a textbook or clinical setting. Now it was in my kitchen and belonged to my husband.

The biggest problem with Brooks' story was that he believed it, and he wanted me to believe it too. My husband, who was looking more like his old self on the outside every day, had changed on the inside forever. He wasn't supposed to act like a patient. This was not "sweet," and the definition of "better" that worked at the hospital seemed completely inadequate in the outside world. I wanted Brooks back the way he'd always been.

Before Brooks became ill, our lives had been a demanding and intricate dance, choreographed to incorporate our careers, our children, and our many interests, and taking a lot of energy to sustain. Brooks wanted a wife to spend time with him, and because of his professional interests, he was gone a great deal of the time. My children alternated between school and home, and when Brooks was home, his kids were usually with us too, so the number of children fluctuated from zero to six on a regular basis. Meanwhile, I maintained my professional responsibilities, dealt with all of the normal household chores, and kept up with community activities. "Dogs, kids, and rock and roll," Brooks used to say when describing our day-to-day existence. I liked the rhythm.

For relaxation, we traveled, and during those times, Brooks took over. His experience as a pilot and his skill at navigating the intricacies of any excursion gave me a chance to sit back, relax, and recharge my batteries. I loved these opportunities to be the sidekick, to take a break with no responsibilities.

Standing in the kitchen that day, in the midst of this strange homecoming, I realized that my sidekick breaks were over. This pilot, who had delighted in finding the way to points unknown for both of us, could no longer visualize an efficient way to get from point A to point B. This man who had a clear understanding of the world and whose words I could always rely on, this person whom I thought was the most intellectually honest being I had ever met, was confused, but he didn't know he was confused. To add insult to injury, he wanted me to react as I always had: with acceptance of what he said and affirmation that I could trust his words.

As I stood there gazing at my husband, I felt alone in a whole new way. Wherever I looked, I saw work. Wherever I looked, I saw chaos. And I had no clue what to do next. So I went to the store and bought milk. (I don't even drink milk, but at the time, just getting out of the house seemed like a basic survival strategy.)

In the days and weeks to come, I muddled along. I put one foot in front of the other, stepping around sadness, struggling with chaos and fear, dodging rage, and wading through grief, until I found a path. Eventually that path led me back to myself, to Brooks, and to a new us.

Of course, when he had dizzy spells or headaches, my

fear would return, and my mind would revisit the trauma of the previous months. As he recovered and learned what had happened to him—he had to learn it many times over because he had no memory of the actual events—Brooks, too, came to fear the onset of ominous symptoms.

Brooks' awareness made me feel that I was no longer alone in my concern, and in a way this was strangely comforting. But he had seen many battles, and he knew how to hold his fear in check and keep moving forward. I had no choice but to follow. I respected his courage too much to fail him.

• • •

Although it was frustrating when Brooks couldn't remember, there were times when his memory loss was a *good* thing—for example, when he (who had no recollection of the last time we'd made love) wanted to resume our sex life immediately after leaving the hospital (well, at least immediately after I got the milk).

The doctors had said they had no clue what would happen when Brooks resumed normal activities. "Go ahead and try things," they'd advised. Taking that advice, I had decided that we would plunge ahead, and each time Brooks lived through a new adventure, I would view his success as passing some kind of "stress test."

Sex wasn't exactly the first such test I had in mind. Nevertheless, on the unmade bed in the cluttered bedroom, with weeks of mail spilling onto the floor from the kitchen table and the carcass of the naked Christmas tree adding an eerie decorating touch, Brooks passed his first stress test. I, on the other hand, felt as if I might have my own medical crisis, but I, too, survived, and we began to begin again.

CHAPTER 7
Change

"If you want things to change, change what you are doing."
Robin Sharma

- We can only change ourselves and we must be inside the loop if we want to effect change in an organization or institution.

- We can try to set up situations that foster change, we can model accepting change, but in the end, real change must come from within us.

- Sometimes the hardest thing to do is "walk away" —to realize we may have to accept what others decide about change.

- Walking away may be the outward expression of change within.

Although we loved our home, as the months went by, it no longer fit our new reality. I wanted to assume more of my professional life, but I didn't want to leave Brooks alone for long periods of time. A friend found us the perfect solution in an old Victorian mansion with an office in the back where I could work.

The owners needed house sitters while they traveled for a couple of years and we moved into the largest house we had ever seen. The foyer was larger than many houses, with an incredible winding staircase out of some Ginger Rogers/Fred Astaire movie. One room was chartreuse, another purple, still another aqua and everywhere the walls were covered with interesting and exotic art.

The kitchen, designed for the days when long-ago occupants had servants, was huge, and the dining room boasted a table that could seat 30.

For an added decorative touch, tall stalks of ancient orchids filled many windows and the kids thought the house would make a great place for a Halloween party.

To get ready for the move, I gave the kids a lot of stuff and staged a garage sale to dispose of the remainder. JC, David, and some friends helped load the moving truck, and with Christy at our side and Willie Nelson playing Brooks' favorite song on the radio, we were "on the road again."

Shortly after we settled into our new digs, Brooks asked, for the second time, about returning to work. A pilot's license is based on medical tests, and I knew he would never qualify again. Because of his memory problems, I also knew he didn't remember that he'd asked this question before.

As time went on, one of the most difficult things for me was to keep my mouth shut, letting Brooks misunderstand things until he was ready to understand them. So I'd been quiet when he'd told his buddies of his plans to return to work. When they looked at me to see if I would correct him, I didn't return their glance. I let it be, knowing, or at least hoping, that someday Brooks would make enough progress to understand the situation. One day he did, and it was a sad day.

Once again we were in a power struggle. This time the struggle was not with the forces of the universe, but with Brooks himself. I'll take the universe any day. An independent and powerful man, Brooks had rarely experienced restrictions on his life. Now his life included many restrictions. He could not fly. He could not ski. He could not ride his motorcycle, and most of the time, he could not find his way from point A to point B in our new home. From his perspective, his wife, the person closest to him, was attempting to rein him in. Although I had tried to help him understand the reasons behind some of his restrictions, in spite of my best intentions, he felt he was in prison, and clearly, I was the warden.

Brooks wanted to go to Denver, to visit Andy, then on to Utah. It was nearing winter again, almost ski season. His doctors, however, had advised him to avoid high altitudes. No one knew for sure, but they believed the reduced atmospheric pressure could allow greater expansion of the blood vessels, thus increasing the chance of another hemorrhage. Although by this time Brooks had been cleared by his doctors to drive, we had been fighting about this trip for days, and I was in shock when I came home and realized he'd left for Colorado alone in his 1986 red Toyota pickup truck.

I was weary, sad, and lost, but I also couldn't help but laugh at the absurdity of the situation. After all, it was only Brooks' short-term memory that was impaired. He had driven to Denver dozens of times in the past, and with his long-term memory intact, he probably had a better shot at finding Denver than finding the kitchen. Obviously, Brooks taking off for Colorado wasn't very smart, but it *was* very Brooks, and this left me both frightened and hopeful. Clearly, he was trying to find himself again.

I sat in the bedroom of our unfamiliar house, surrounded by brightly colored walls covered with global artifacts, and looked at the old rotary phone with its thin, brittle cord. I looked at that phone for a long time, trying to decide whether to call the police or resign as warden and turn in my "keys." Finally, I decided to stop fighting to save him and let him go. Right or wrong, on some level Brooks had to define life on his terms, and I had to unlock the cell that was killing him. Still, my heart broke when he called me from the road to say, "I am a truck driver, and I am going to sleep on the side of the road." The pain numbed my soul when he called again to say that the farther he got from me, the better he felt.

At last the call came from Andy: Brooks was in danger, but he had made it to Denver, no one was hurt, and he was still alive.

Brooks had been dizzy and nauseated when he reached Denver, with dangerously high blood pressure. Andy took him to the hospital, where he was seen immediately.

By the time my plane arrived in Denver the next day, Brooks had been released from the hospital and was staying with Andy in the "keg room" of a rowdy, college-guy, nightmare of a house that made our mansion seem more or less simple. Andy shared the place with five other students, and the basement keg room, which reeked of stale beer from too many parties, was the only unoccupied space.

Brooks had enough sense to tell Andy, "I don't think your mother is going to want to stay here," and he was right, but it was the weekend of the Pope's visit to the mile-high city. Since we needed all the help we could get, I sort of liked the timing until I realized that, as a result, there were no hotel rooms in the Denver area.

The doctors wanted Brooks to stay in town for a few days so they could watch him. Fortunately, since Brooks was a retired Lt. Colonel in the Marine Corps Reserve, I was able to secure lodging for us at a local Air Force base. Until the doctors said Brooks could go home, we lived in an apartment for visiting officers. (While there, Brooks, this man who had cheated death in the air many times, let down his guard long enough to admit he was wrong, that he never should have made the trip, and that worst of all, he had been afraid he was going to die in the keg room.)

Finally we were allowed to head out, but as I drove us home in his pickup, my newfound compassion had diminished considerably, and I was not a happy camper. The seats were hard, the ride was bumpy, the radio didn't work, and I was so mad that steam poured from my ears (or so I imagined).

We were quiet until we reached Nebraska, hundreds of silent miles from Denver. Silence is not our normal style, and I think we both were deafened by its presence. Finally, I turned and looked at Brooks, this man-child of mine. Unable to connect with him in the old ways, I did what millions of kids do when they have no good responses. I turned to him and crossed my eyes, contorting my face into some kind of silly mask. My message, child to child, spoke of my frustrations at the ridiculousness of our situation and my lack of understanding about where to start again. Brooks, by this time realizing he'd pushed me as far as I could stretch, and probably more, that he had pushed himself as far as he could reach, got the message. He accepted my childish gesture with its message of powerlessness and its offer of a truce. A wordless but powerful connection crackled between us, and we began to laugh. We laughed at life, at his frustrations and mine. We laughed at being crazy, at our own insanity. We laughed about hating each other. We laughed at ourselves. We laughed at Andy's keg room, and we drove on.

What had begun as a flight from reality became a trip

with a new destination. On that flat prairie highway, with miles of bumps, potholes, and dangerous curves ahead of us, heading back to our Halloween house and its chartreuse walls, Brooks began his long journey home.

CHAPTER 8
Growth

"Since feelings come first, he who listens to the syntax
of things will never wholly kiss me."
T. S. Eliot

When searching for a psychotherapist I consider the following....

- Mental health clinicians, including psychologists, social workers, psychiatrists, and counselors, are licensed by the state in which they practice. Licensure means they have passed some tests of knowledge and are expected to work within ethical guidelines.

- These therapists work within a theoretical model. We call it a modality. Individual therapists subscribe to the theories of Beck, Freud, Jung, Skinner, Sullivan, Maslow, Lazarus, Erickson, Seligman, and many others.

- It is important to understand the modality of the therapist with whom you choose to work.

- The relationship between the therapist and the client is another powerful force and an important part of the platform upon which progress is built.

As a graduate student, I had learned about brain injuries. After such an injury, my professors had taught that the brain could recover, to whatever extent possible, for about two years. After that, not much would change.

By the time we returned from Denver, I needed a greater understanding of this process than my dated textbooks could provide. Although I had learned much during my years of practice, and had taught psychology classes, I was by no means an expert on brain injuries. Fortunately, Mia had a childhood friend who was now a practicing neuropsychologist. This generous young woman sent me several new textbooks on brain rehabilitation, and I began to read.

Apparently things had changed since my graduate school days. Experts now understood the brain to be much more elastic than they had first believed. It turns out that people aren't "stuck" at the level of functioning they attain by some arbitrary two-year mark. In fact, they can continue to recover for as long as they live.

Reading these books was exciting. It had been a long time since I'd been involved in a research project. Now I had my own private project: Brooks!

I knew the brain held as many mysteries as actual, proven "facts," so I decided to take some chances and see what worked. I'd like to say I knew beyond a shadow of a doubt how much progress was possible, but the truth is, I had no idea. I knew how Brooks used to be, knew that he probably wasn't going to be like that again, but beyond these basic facts, I had no clue what to expect. The one thing I did know was that we had nothing to lose by trying.

So I enrolled Brooks in every formal rehabilitation program I could find. He worked with a fellow who had patterns to follow and rearrange on a computer. The patterns were of all shapes and sizes, and working with them required concentration. Brooks found this mildly interesting, and this nice-guy psychologist also cared about the rest of Brooks' life.

Unfortunately, the patterns in the rest of Brooks' life included getting lost walking around town and experiencing periods of intense frustration at having no job, no goals, and no reliable short-term memory. He seemed very sad, and these feelings, coupled with his brain injury, contributed to his overwhelming fatigue. He was no longer able to run or to engage in any of the vigorous sports at which he had once excelled. He was just too damn tired, and a lot of the time, he was too damn mad.

Next, I found a psychologist to help Brooks with his frustration and depression. She was a nice woman, with an interest in helping him with day-to-day living. She tried to explain to him that, even though it was hard for him to believe he was confused or incorrect in some of his thoughts, it would be a good idea to try to listen to those of us who saw things from another angle. (Dream on, girl.) She also tried to explain that it was necessary for me to do the driving when we went out, and for him to rage at me because of this fact was not good for either of us. She pleaded with him to believe me when I explained the best route from point A to point B. (Sure, like that would happen.)

Brooks had spent most of his adult life as either a single pilot in a small fighter jet, doing loops and twirls that would make the rest of us ill, or in his airline work as the "left seat" person—the captain. Now he had been demoted. I was in the left seat and he was in the right, and this juxtaposition forced him to look his changed circumstances squarely in the eye. When confronted with his new reality, Brooks reacted like any human animal: His "flight-or-fight" response kicked in, and flight was not a style taught in the United States Marine Corps.

Even without allowing for a brain injury, it is well documented that men and women look at directions differently. Men tend to give directions by referring to north, south, east, or west, while women more often use landmarks. You know, "Go to the red house and turn left; when you come to the wheelbarrow full of flowers, go right."

In most cases, I believe that men and women are more alike than different—we are, in fact, both from Earth—but when it comes to directions, I bow to the documentation. And as for how Brooks and I viewed directions: Before his illness we might have been from different planets, but now we were from entirely different universes.

Brooks always had been skilled at finding his way. I had been known to get lost in parking garages. To compensate, before setting out on a journey, I wrote down every landmark, every turn. Before his illness, Brooks thought this approach foolish, and before his illness, for him it would have been. Unfortunately, he now considered my obsessive study before each trip a sign of my lack of confidence in his ability, which of course was absolutely true. Every time we entered a car, my stomach was in knots. There was something about being in that small space, with my husband either yelling at me or fuming silently (which was every bit as loud), that to this day can send me off in search of antacids.

As the "which way do we go" arguments began to permeate most aspects of our life together, it felt as if every muscle in my body was in a permanent state of tension. I knew I needed help in getting through to Brooks, or maybe I just needed help. *This cannot continue or we will both be dead*, I thought in my more melodramatic moments.

My girlfriends have often asked me, "I said the same thing to my husband that you said to him. Why will he listen to you and not listen to me?"

I've always replied (only partly joking), "I don't know, but my husband is the same. If I really need him to understand and agree with an issue, I have someone else tell him."

In reality, Brooks and I had great respect for each other. Respect and trust formed the foundation on which our marriage was built. We saw ourselves as equals, different in our strengths, but balanced by respect and personal power. Now, all bets were off.

We still clung to the remnants of respect, but on a day-to-day basis, neither of us believed the other. Brooks had created an alternate reality, especially about directions, that was not on any map I had ever seen, and he was somewhat correct in his conviction that I never had been able to read a map properly anyway, so why should he believe me now.

Of course, the fact that Brooks was impaired in his directional reasoning did not mean that my abilities magically improved. Necessity, however, sometimes produces amazing results. After awhile I got better at figuring out how to get from one place to another, which then presented the next problem: Neither of us dared to believe me.

I was so new at trusting my increasing directional skill that it didn't take much argument from Brooks to make me believe I was wrong. Then I would cave in and let him guide us, only to discover that his skills didn't match his confidence. My stomach would clutch as I realized my mistake, told him I was going a different way, and then sat captive as his rage permeated the car. I had fantasies of jumping out of the car and perhaps out of my life.

Our nice-lady psychologist tried to discuss these issues with Brooks, but honestly, he held her in lower esteem than me. This sexist pilot, accustomed to being in charge of everything that had an engine and many things that didn't, had no respect for anyone with a rank lower than his. For whatever reason, he saw the two of us as equals—probably because I would have it no other way. But I knew that if he could have admitted it without me jumping down his throat, he generally trusted men more than women.

And so, giving in to reality, I decided that perhaps the key to getting Brooks to listen to my point of view would be to find a psychologist he would be more likely to respect: a psychologist like him. A psychologist with a penis.

As a cognitive behaviorist, I believe in an approach to therapy—a modality—that takes into account thoughts, feelings, and behaviors. As a person who also believes in the effectiveness of positive psychology, I teach people to find and use their strengths so they can move forward to discover their passion and what Seligman calls their "authentic selves." I am a teacher. I believe in goals, skills, hard work, and opportunity. Other therapists believe in other modalities. There are lots of theories as to the best modality, and the trick is to match the right treatment and the right therapist with the right client.

Research tells us that one of the most important issues in therapy, with respect to change or improvement, is the relationship between the client and the therapist. So I decided to put aside my personal beliefs and go on a hunt for a psychologist with whom Brooks could relate. I must admit my bias, though: I did hunt for a cognitive behaviorist with a penis.

I also decided this therapist needed stripes on his shoulders. Since psychologists, unlike pilots, don't rank themselves this way, or at least not in public, perhaps it would be best to find an *old* male cognitive behavioral psychologist. Would Brooks equate age with stripes?

I was on a roll. Next I decided it was important for this

person to have high status—a tenured professor would be good (although there was the problem that Brooks thought anyone who usually kept his feet on the ground was somewhat inadequate). Could there possibly be an old male cognitive behavioral psychologist professor who could fly a plane or who had fought in a war?

A least I was narrowing the field.

At the end of my search, I settled on a well-respected professor with a lot of life experience. He met many, if not all, of my other criteria, and I arranged for Brooks to meet with him on a regular basis. At times, I joined them.

Ever the organized wife, I often sent Brooks off to his therapy sessions with suggestions of things to work on, and, sadly, Brooks tried to please me. When I was asked to send in a list of what I wanted from this therapy, and I realized my list contained 624 items, I knew I had lost it. The truth is, there was only one thing I wanted: my husband back.

Brooks and the psychologist met for a few months, but little changed. Despite the therapist's skill, Brooks was not invested in the process. In addition, because of his short-term memory loss, he couldn't recall most of what they'd talked about, anyway. The reality was, Brooks had lost his dignity, his self-respect, and his future, as well as his memory, and it was going to take much more than therapy to make things right again.

My dynamic, self-confident spouse had gone from being a hotshot fighter pilot, a drop-dead-handsome international airline captain, and a responsible husband and father, to a man who couldn't sleep through the night, couldn't concentrate, and was either tired or mad, and sometimes both. Imagine his feelings when he was confused in his own home, lost in his new neighborhood, and couldn't find his way to the airport. Think of the frustration he must have experienced when he incurred the wrath of his wife just for insisting he knew what he was talking about.

Other people treated him differently. Instead of slapping him on the back with a vote of confidence in his success and bright future, they talked to him as if he were a patient. "Hey, man, where'd you go this week?" was replaced with, "Hello, Brooks. How are you feeling?" Both words and tone reflected his new status. People treated him as a "less than," and he knew it.

My behavior was different, too. I no longer went on my merry way, expecting him to do the same. I followed him around. I alternated between babying him and being mad at him. I accused him of trying to make things harder. I didn't trust him to give me accurate information or to take care of himself. We still were engaged with each other, and we were sometimes adversaries, but we were no longer equals.

I had to find a way to help him—and me for that matter. Somehow we had to go forward, forward toward something for which, at that time, I had no vision.

A future for me, with goals and dreams, was not on my radar screen. *I* was not on my radar screen. Instead, I had become an extension of Brooks. I disapproved of this model for my life, but Brooks needed an extension. He had wrapped himself in self-protection and couldn't reach out to the world on his own.

My self-protection was anger. Generally, I'm not a very angry person. I tend to understand situations, am solution-based, and usually don't take things personally. However, in this case, I think I stayed angry at Brooks as a way to propel us both forward. If I remained angry, it was an outward manifestation of my determination not to accept the status quo, and it was a signal to Brooks that he was going to have to work harder.

I also was very vocal. I yelled at Brooks at home and I yelled at him in the car. I went to therapy with him and yelled at him there, and then I yelled at the therapists. I used my rage to tell them all they were inadequate.

Luckily for me, these competent professionals understood. I believe they probably knew I couldn't back down and accept the current reality as the end of the road for Brooks. Or maybe they were afraid of my wrath: I am a powerful woman. *In any event, no one took me on and tried to get me to give up my anger and grieve, and for that I will be forever grateful. It wasn't yet time to grieve, and to have had it forced on me would have been a disaster for Brooks and me.*

I am keenly aware that human beings are born resilient, hard-wired to withstand and even flourish in the face of adversity. Don't get me wrong: Poverty, abuse, racism, neglect, and repeated trauma all are factors that can impair our natural resilience. By the same token, there are many skills and strategies we can use to enhance our innate resilience. If this were not so, our species would not be here today.

Believing in this innate ability, I teach people the skills to enhance their natural resilience. Moreover, I'm convinced people will deal with things when *they* are ready— within *their* time frame, not mine, and that they'll use the skills they've learned to move forward at a pace uniquely right for them. Growth happens from within, and I believe that while it is important to learn skills and strategies to go forward in life, it is equally important to respect your feelings and understand the time frame in which to use them.

I'm a thinker. I think my way through tough times. I'm fairly intuitive, in touch with my deeper feelings, and usually aware when I'm choosing not to deal with them. So I knew I was using anger to cover my grief, but it just didn't seem like the time to grieve. In the overall scheme of things, it was obvious that Brooks' losses were far bigger than mine, and I felt that attending to my own needs would be abandoning him.

I know self-care is important. I talk about it all the time. But I also know there is no such thing as pure altruism: Everything we do benefits us in some way. I didn't expect Brooks or anyone else to think of me as a saint. I am not a saint; in fact, I am fairly hedonistic. I am by nature an optimistic and happy person, and I like a good life.

The truth is, putting Brooks' needs over mine *was* a way to take care of myself. So, I held on to my anger and used the energy it gave me to keep pushing him. This would not have worked forever, but for a brief time, it was the fuel that drove us forward, and I rode this energy like a rocket, hoping it would catapult us into a new universe of possibility.

Brooks is a smart guy, and when he climbed aboard the rocket with me, I think it was for several reasons. First of all, it was the only ride he was offered. Secondly, he had always been happy to ride off into the wild blue yonder. And lastly, he didn't want his current condition to be the end of the road for him, either. Paradoxically, and without words, I knew what Brooks wanted. And so, fueled by my anger and propelled by his, we continued our wild ride into the future.

CHAPTER 9

Humanity

"Experience is a hard teacher.
She gives the test first and the lesson later."
Anonymous

- Great teachers are listeners who teach through their humanity.

- Lives can be changed by the power of a teacher who takes the time to listen and care.

- We are all both teachers and students.

The seasons morphed from winter into spring, from summer toward fall. The classes at our local university were starting, and one day, after watching Brooks sleep all afternoon, listening to the phone never ring for him, seeing his drifting sorrow at having no schedule or goals, I had an idea. Brooks needed more to do than rearrange patterns on a computer screen at the rehab center, or go to therapy to try to please a wife whom he had been able to please before by his mere presence. I would send him to school.

The university in our town was within walking distance of our Halloween house. Brooks had gone to Stanford. While it's true he had been more of a party animal and athletic star than an academic, and he calls his geology major "rocks for jocks," the fact is that he managed (although he likes to joke about how it was a close call) to graduate in a *mere* five years. Despite his lack of early academic prowess, however, Brooks had achieved a lot of success in life, and I knew he was a secret intellectual. A voracious reader and an expert in many fields, he was especially interested in guns, planes, war, and politics. Brooks and I share a love of history, and we have argued about politics since the night we met.

Given his interests, the next step in my plan seemed a natural one: I called up a professor at the university who was an expert on the Civil War. His lectures were famous for their brilliance. I had never met him, and I didn't know anyone who knew him. I looked him up in the phone book and, to my amazement, he was not only listed but he answered my call, and when he did, I poured out my story. I told him of my wonderful husband, a man about his age, who had lost many of the supports that the rest of us use to define ourselves. I told him of Brooks' sadness, of his passion for history, and of his need for a challenge he could meet. I asked the professor if there were any way Brooks could become his student. I knew the university had formal methods to audit classes, but I didn't know them, and the beginning of the fall term was only a few days away.

This kind stranger listened to me and said, "Send him over. He can be in my lecture class." Hope continued to move in, changing from an occasional visitor to a permanent resident in my heart.

As I thought about this new opportunity for Brooks, I had a vision. I could see him becoming an expert on the Civil War. I visualized the day he received his masters, then his doctorate. My mind's eye filled with joy as I saw him accept his graduate diplomas. Then I said, "Hold on, Teena," and returned to reality. (I am always off and running in my dreams.) "One day at a time," I reminded myself. "This must be for Brooks, done his way, if it is to help." It was not easy for me to stuff my aspirations—it never is—but I knew this must be about Brooks, and on his terms.

With hope in my heart and joy in my step, I walked with Brooks to class that first day, knowing he couldn't find his way alone. It reminded me of the first day of school for each of my children, when I had felt that same sense of love, hope, and excitement. He was excited too. This Marine had a mission.

Within days Brooks *did* find his way, both to class and back. In fact, that fall he learned to walk many places in town: to the bookstore for his textbooks, to the café for lunch, to the barbershop. He loved his class, he loved the professor, and he loved learning. He finally had a reason to struggle, a reason to find a new direction, and his self-worth lay at the end of the path.

He brought home books to read. It took him hours to finish a chapter, but he was captivated by the material. So what if he couldn't remember anything the next day? He was happy to read each chapter again and again.

After awhile, when the infrequent phone calls came from his friends, the conversation changed from the exploits of others and a concern for Brooks' health to questions about his classes. His buddies, top competitors all, started talking about Brooks' growing expertise. More calls came. As friends and family supported him in his new and eventually encompassing interest, our home filled with Civil War memorabilia. His reading became easier, and his walk to class had an urgency of expectation. One day he actually spoke in class, and then again, and soon his questions and answers were seen as so insightful that he was asked to join a study group with the other students.

As months grew into years, we visited every Civil War site you can imagine. I learned more about Grant, Lee, Jackson, Stuart, and my personal favorite, Joshua Chamberlain, than I ever wanted to know. I drove Brooks to sites of Civil War battles I never knew existed. I listened as he explained the strategy behind each attack or retreat, and within the context of this era of history that had never held that much interest for me, I began to see traces of my husband again, the man he had been before the hemorrhage. He would appear on the battlefields of Gettysburg, on the road to Richmond, and in the car as we listened to tapes describing the struggles that once had raged on the quiet expanses of green before us.

I was excited by each brief visit with the Brooks of old, and sad when he retreated into himself. But I knew he was there, and I looked forward to our next time together. I actually saw these occasions as dates. It was the only way I could protect myself. It was too upsetting to expect rapid change. And so I looked forward to the next "date," even if I had to travel across the Mason-Dixon line to have it.

As time went on, Brooks became more and more like his old self, expanding his interests to encompass the Revolutionary War and then to topics that didn't include war at all—a big relief for me.

One focus of his broadening interest was Lewis and Clark. On the road again, we visited many of the sites along their historic journey. I even moved some of the Civil War trinkets to make room for the Lewis and Clark paraphernalia that was filling our life. Eventually I decided I didn't need to know another fact about Lewis, Clark, their brilliant female guide, Sackajawea, the Civil War, or the Revolutionary War. Brooks' needs were lessening.

I was, however, eager to learn more about my husband, or maybe eager to relearn what I had known before, and eventually I got my wish. During those months of studying about how our nation expanded, split, and then healed again, Brooks began to heal, too. He was different from before, but he was functioning at a very high level, surpassing any prognosis given by any doctor since that first, cold December night. His mood improved, his humor returned, and he was retaining the information he was learning. His depression began to retreat, and with it departed my anger.

The history professor had given Brooks what no medicine could provide, what no therapist could create, what no wife could instill. This learned man, who understood both history and life, gave Brooks a precious gift, a gift that all of us need if we are to flourish. The gift was opportunity: a chance to use his strengths, to follow a passion, to make mistakes in a protected setting, to share his newfound knowledge with others, to rebuild his self-esteem, and to have a purpose worth getting up for each day.

I think often of this man whom I still have never met. He is brilliant, but it was not his great intellect that made the difference. He is famous, but it was not his prestige or status that we needed. Rather, in the simple act of not rebuffing me when I poured out my tale of woe, he set in motion a chain of events that changed the direction of Brooks' life, of my life, and of our future together. When almost everything in Brooks' world had collapsed under the weight of his disabilities, this kind professor gave him a structure to hold onto, and in doing so, gave him back his dignity.

Soon changes on the outside led to deep and lasting changes on the inside. Brooks began to loosen his grip on fear, inadequacy, humiliation, rage, and sadness. The rocket ship had landed, and we had achieved yet another "new" normal. Brooks was now safe enough and well enough for me to think about my own sense of loss and direct my energies toward myself.

CHAPTER 10
Choices

---

*"If of all thy worldly goods thou art bereft
And only two loaves of bread to thee are left,
Sell one; and with the dole
Buy hyacinths to feed thy soul."*
Author Unknown

- It is very difficult to engage in true altruism.

- Often, when we think we are doing something solely for another, if we look closely, we will find that we too are benefiting from our actions.

- If we understand that there is some benefit for us in most of what we choose to do, then we do not have to look to the world for appreciation, because we know we are actually working in our own best interests.

- Recognizing this concept allows us to take responsibility for our choices and go forward with gratitude instead of expectation.

Grief is different from everyday sadness or depression, and it can express itself in many forms. In my case, it took the form of "letting go," of allowing myself to feel the hole in my heart.

For all of my outgoing nature, when it comes to my deep feelings, I am fairly private. As a result, most people didn't know when I was grieving. If someone knew me well, they might have noticed that I was a little less funny, not quite as bright and cheerful, and, at least for me, somewhat quieter, but that was all. I was not depressed, but in the quiet moments, I was in touch with my loss.

I didn't feel sorry for myself; I just don't think that way. In fact, I have always considered myself one of the most fortunate people ever to walk the face of the Earth. I've had that feeling of gratitude from my earliest years and often joke that perhaps I was born with an extra measure of serotonin, the neurotransmitter that gives us our sense of well-being. Or maybe my appreciation of life was shaped by my father's sister Evelyn, whom I barely knew but who sent me Norman Vincent Peale newsletters extolling "the power of positive thinking" starting when I was in the sixth grade. She knew I loved to read, that I would memorize the ingredients off the cereal box if nothing else was available. In retrospect, perhaps she also knew she was throwing me a powerful lifeline, one I could hold onto, when needed, for the rest of my life.

My grief didn't take me to the place where I thought the world had been unfair, or that I deserved more, because

I don't believe any of us deserves anything. The trick is to give.

• • •

I was fortunate to have been born in a time rich with opportunity. As long as I can remember, I have loved to learn and have found teachers to guide me, beginning in the rural farming community where I grew up and continuing until today. As a child, any deficits in my nuclear family were more than made up for by a community that reached out to nurture me through my growing years and by my grandma, who set an example that I cherish. I also had my mom. Grandma had been gone for decades, and Mom had passed away two years before Brooks became ill, but now I found myself missing them both with a renewed intensity.

My grandmother, Martha Harbin Thomas Roberts, spent her youth picking tobacco in the fields of West Virginia. When she married, she moved to Ohio to escape the floods she so hated in the West Virginia countryside. Her first husband passed away when she was still in her twenties; she married again. Between both husbands, she bore a total of seven children. Two of them died in childhood.

When her second husband, my grandpa, died suddenly, Grandma was 34 years old and seven months pregnant with my mother. She never dated again.

After Grandpa's death, Grandma was forced to leave the land they had worked as tenant farmers, but she kept her family together by moving to the county seat of the mid-western farm-belt area where I grew up. Once there, she began a decades-long career as a cook in the kitchens of area restaurants and hotels.

She was a tough, no-nonsense, religious woman, and I never heard her complain. Yet it wasn't until I was an adult that I understood the extent of her sacrifices. At one point I discovered that, for many years during mid-life, Grandma didn't even own a dress. Every penny she made went into supporting her family, so each Saturday night she would wash out her cook's uniform, starch and press the stiff white fabric, and wear it to her Baptist church the next morning. I can still see her walking into that church with her head held high, confident in her belief that all are equal in the eyes of God.

When I learned the story about Grandma not owning a dress, it broke my heart. But it also brought me back to those weekends when my parents would drop me off at the kitchen of the local hotel where Grandma worked. When she finished her shift, the two of us would take a cab to her second-floor, one-room apartment, where I would spend the night. But first, she would let me fix her hair, apply makeup to her face, and choose outlandish outfits for her to wear. Looking back, I imagine she enjoyed this grown-up version of playing "dress-up," a far cry from the life she had known when her own children were young.

Grandma and I were very different people. She thought I was too loud, too opinionated, talked too much, and didn't clean my room enough. I was not her favorite grandchild. However, she was my only grandparent and we worked it out, because neither of us had a choice. Gratefully, she lived long enough for me to share with her some of life's luxuries. Once I took her to New York City to see the sights and enjoy some Broadway shows. At Sardi's, one of the fancy restaurants I thought she might enjoy, she ordered stewed tomatoes and nothing else. She was true to herself, and I admired her grit (long before I understood the meaning of authenticity).

My mother, Urban Eileen Roberts Long Ellery, was the youngest of Grandma's girls. A secretary by day and small-town lounge singer by night, she was funny, entertaining, and a beautiful young woman. She had blond hair and blue eyes and wanted me to be Miss America or a movie star, her vision of success.

Most of her life, Mother had been babied by Grandma and her four older half-sisters. All of this attention created a trap for her, but I could see it was a trap from which she chose not to break free. Not wanting to join her in the same situation, I approached life in a different way.

To my mother's chagrin, I had neither blond hair nor blue eyes nor any interest in becoming Miss America. Even worse, I wasn't good at singing or dancing. Instead, I loved schoolwork, loved to read, hated cigarettes (both her passion and the cause of her premature death), and dreaded the weekend nights when she consumed too much beer. We had many differences, but still I knew she loved me, and eventually we were able to accept and forgive one another for being who we were.

As a child, I looked forward to those Sundays when our extended family gathered around the piano Grandma had sent to our home (without Mom's knowledge) because she thought I should learn to play. I loved my aunts' piano playing, my mom's singing and playfulness on these occasions, and the feeling of belonging to these strong, connected women, each of whom worked outside the home. They were a solid, working-class group, and I couldn't wait to hear their stories of intrigue at work and at home. From time to time, Mom and the aunts would fight tooth and nail, but they always made up to form a solid block of protection for each other against the outside world. And Grandma led the way.

As my grief took me back in time to my roots in Ohio, I remembered those feelings of comfort from my childhood, the lessons learned, and the strategies admired. Those were some of the times I cried. I longed for that comfort and kindness, but I was learning to comfort myself, and in time I started to feel better.

I have always loved to work. I fall into bed at night tired but like to relax by reading or watching some television. Now I found myself obsessed with David Letterman. My choice of programs was not a conscious decision: I think I just liked his form of comfort. He made me laugh. So every night I would sit in bed laughing at Letterman, driving Brooks crazy as he was trying, unsuccessfully, to get to sleep. Frustrated, he bought me a plug to stick into the TV so I could listen with earphones. Now Brooks slept, and I laughed, and after awhile I no longer cried or missed the comforts of the past. I was living in the moment.

One day, after I'd been laughing at Letterman for some months, I went shopping. I hadn't shopped in awhile and I needed new clothes. I remember seeing these soft, cotton knit suits with short or long skirts, mock turtlenecks, and free-form jackets. I bought some in varying lengths and different colors—red, black, and eggplant. My shopping spree served my practical needs, but it also was a sign of awakening. Once again I had found myself, separate from Brooks. Soon I began to laugh even more in the daytime, as well as with my friend David Letterman at night. Looking back, I can see that I was laughing my way back to myself.

About this time, Mia made an announcement. She and Matt, a young man she had met in law school, had decided to marry. We loved Matt and were excited about this great event. But in all honesty, my joy was tempered by concern about how I was going to do it all and give my beloved daughter a fun wedding.

I shouldn't have worried. Mia makes any situation fun.

As plans started to gel, everyone cooperated. My former husband and his wife, Matt's parents, and Brooks and I all worked together to help the kids plan the event. The wedding was scheduled for New Year's Eve.

Mia was finishing her doctorate in Wisconsin, Matt was working with a large international organization in

Vienna, Austria, and I was busy with my changing life. In spite of these complicated logistics, everything came together, guests arrived from several states and continents, and it was time to party.

Preparing for this party triggered memories of another New Year's celebration, one from when I was a little girl and my dad, a factory worker, was on strike. His paycheck stopped, and he walked the picket line for many months. That year, Mom, too lost her job, and we came close to losing our home. When the holidays came around, the union gave us a ham. Instead of cooking it for our Christmas meal, however, Mom saved it and had a party on New Year's Eve. She could have chosen to wallow in despair, to give in to her fear, to forget the holidays, but Mom was a little oppositional. Sometimes she wasn't pointed in the right direction, but she had a fierce determination, and although we were different in many ways, this was one characteristic we shared. And so on that New Year's Eve, about to attend my daughter's wedding (a fiercely determined woman in her own right), I thanked Mom with all my heart for what she had taught me.

Matt's mom is an elegant European and former diplomat in the French government. She is regal, an expert in opera, and a very cultured woman. His dad, a former surgeon and still-practicing physician in Denver, matches her in stature. Matt's parents are now our close friends, but before the wedding I was a little embarrassed about our transient living situation. Then I remembered Mom and

Grandma, and when Matt's folks arrived, I welcomed them warmly, along with everyone else, into our Halloween house with its chartreuse and aqua walls, exotic furniture, and "Little Shop of Horrors" windows festooned with orchids.

The wedding took place at an old inn located in the center of our town. The kids had asked Brooks to do a reading, and there wasn't a dry eye in the house when, standing in his rented tuxedo and wearing his favorite cowboy boots—ever the cowboy in his heart—Brooks read a poem he had labored to find and recite perfectly. It was a poem about growing old together, about the riches of love.

Years before, when Brooks first let me know how serious his feelings were for me, he told me how much he wished to grow old with me. At the time I had been a little taken aback. Up until then, I hadn't given much thought to growing old at all, let alone doing it with another person.

Now I knew why he had practiced his reading in secret. On New Year's Eve the year before, Brooks had been near death from the staph infection. That night, standing in front of family, friends, and kids, he sent me a coded message. He intended to get his wish.

Later, when the dancing was over, the plates cleared, the wine bottles drained, and the guests had departed, I sat alone in the empty ballroom of the inn and basked in the joy of the night. The events of the evening sparkled in my mind. At midnight, our town had set off fireworks that we could see from the windows of the ballroom. By then, Mia had spilled wine down the front of her beautiful dress, her wedding slipper had lost a heel, and she was leading the conga line through the inn. As she passed by me, radiant and glowing with joy, and with the rest of our kids laughing as they followed behind, she leaned over and said, "Mom, it doesn't get any better than this!"

In the quiet of that deserted room, I knew she was right. My grieving was over. On a nearby table, I spotted a half-empty bottle of champagne. Before the staff could clear it, I reached over and poured myself a glass. Gazing through the window at the dark winter sky sprinkled with bold, shining lights, I gave thanks for having survived all that had happened, for Brooks' survival, for our kids, and for this glorious night, both an ending and a beginning.

Then I got up and hurried off to bed, because the next morning, scores of wedding guests were coming to the house for breakfast. After all, what was the sense of living in a Halloween house, with its giant dining room and walls of many colors, if I didn't make good use of it?

I served ham.

CHAPTER 11

Strengths

"It's a little like wrestling a gorilla.
You don't quit when you're tired,
you quit when the gorilla is tired."
Robert Strauss

- Recognizing our individual strengths can lead us to our authentic style of leadership.

- Understanding the strengths of others allows us to gain confidence in their abilities, realize our way of leading is not the only way, and learn from them.

- There are as many styles of leadership as there are people who lead.

- Resilience is the platform upon which leadership is built.

There is no such thing as an uneventful year for any of us. I have learned, paradoxically, that "uneventful" is perhaps the most wonderful event of all. The next couple of years fell into that category.

The owners returned to reclaim their house and we moved on. Brooks took up golf, a sport he had disdained before his illness as too boring, but which he now embraced with enthusiasm. We golfed together, Brooks easily out-playing me, and we enjoyed our times together and with the family. No longer Brooks' extension, I watched as he reached out to our kids, nieces, nephews, and the entire family, both dead and alive. Brooks had discovered genealogy—the outward manifestation, perhaps, of his search for himself.

Now that Brooks had both the health and the time to visit with his dad, they spent countless hours looking up long-lost relatives. The relationship between the two of them had always been strained, and with Brooks' mom no longer around to act as mediator, I hoped the time had come when they would talk about the tension between them. Instead, they read the papers together, went out to lunch together, watched TV together, and did what fathers and sons have done for centuries: loved each other without comment. Brooks had lost his mom and almost lost his life. "Grandpa" had lost his wife of 60 years and nearly lost his son. Both men had grown, and their love and appreciation for each other seemed to have grown, too.

Brooks and my stepfather, Charles, had always been close, but now their relationship took on a different dimension, nurtured by their new mutual passion: golf. Whenever they could find a tee time, they hit the links together, then spent countless hours "perfecting" their play by watching golf matches on television.

The entire group—Charles, "Grandpa," and Brooks—functioned as a unit on grandpa-time. Usually the two older men got up early, ate, and read the paper. After Brooks arose and had his breakfast, they all read the paper some more. Then it was time for lunch.

Brooks' medical problems had taken their toll. He could no longer be licensed to fly airplanes, yet all of his buddies still took to the skies. He was retired from the Marine Corps Reserve, but most of the guys he'd served with were in the midst of their careers. It was easy to see why he preferred hanging out with the grandpas. He could be the young one, and he had two loving fathers who both protected and cared for him.

During those years, which I think of as a kind of plateau—not as it used to be and not as it was to become—life was busy, but the background was a hum of sweetness, normalcy, and family. The children continued to mature, earning numerous degrees and acquiring spouses and jobs as they moved into adulthood. I was able to expand my professional life, and when I wasn't working, Brooks and I relaxed, traveled, and enjoyed time together and apart.

One year, we vacationed with Mia and Matt in Spain, where Matt's mom owns a home on a small island. The summer heat of Spain is legendary, but even so, both

Brooks and Mia seemed unwell. I didn't know which one to worry about more. As their symptoms worsened, I remember lying in bed one night, anxiously reviewing all of the illnesses that Mia could have contracted, then wondering why Brooks' gait seemed so slow.

By evening of the following day, Mia's "problem" became clear when the couple announced they were expecting our first grandchild. This proclamation was met by tears all around, especially from Brooks, who becomes almost giddy when he hears of an impending new arrival. I looked at him, touched by his excitement, but aware on another level that his reaction was part of his "life force." This is a man who likes to drive things forward, who favors expansion. He is happiest when his planes are full.

Although Brooks was thrilled by the thought of becoming a grandpa, his step was slower than usual for the remainder of our trip. Then, at a stopover in Heathrow Airport on the way home, he fell. He wasn't dizzy, he said; his left leg just collapsed. I called University Hospital as soon as we landed in the States. "Get him here as soon as possible," they said.

Many tests later, the doctors determined that Brooks had an injury in the neck area of his spinal cord. They believed a combination of arthritis and stenosis (a narrowing in his spinal column) had compressed the cord, causing an interruption to the signals telling his left leg to move. Although spinal cord stenosis is congenital, arthritis in this area is often the result of years of being an athlete.

Brooks had been a high-level athlete from his earliest days. After his hemorrhage, he'd not only had a stroke, he'd also spent months in bed on his back. Brooks' neck had hurt in the hospital, and on that first trip home, he hadn't even been able to hold up his head. The weakness in his left leg was apparently a further manifestation of these problems.

In an attempt to relieve the pressure on the cord and alleviate his growing symptoms, the doctors operated on Brooks within days of our return from Spain. After the surgery, he spent a difficult month of recovery in a rehabilitation hospital. He didn't want to be there and I didn't blame him. After everything he'd gone through, ending up in such a place was tough to take. He had no memory of his cerebral hemorrhage and subsequent months in bed, but now that he was aware of his problems and his status, he hated being a patient.

I had told him many times about his first crisis, the one in which he'd almost died, but even though he'd had to live with the outcome of those events, the events themselves, in some respects, were simply a story to him. Now, fully aware of what was happening in his body, the story became real.

His neck pain was so severe that, once again, he couldn't hold up his head. In rehab he barely spoke, and although he complied with the doctors and nurses, he avoided their gaze and didn't reach out to them. He refused to eat or socialize with the other patients, demanding to take every meal in bed, alone.

When I visited him, we sat in silence. He was mad at me, but I didn't take it personally. He was mad at everyone, and I had learned to respect his silence. The only thing I could do that seemed to give him any joy was bring him food. Yet upon my next visit, I often found the food uneaten, still in its wrapper on the nightstand next to his bed.

Brooks said he hated the doctors, the therapists, the aides, and the other patients, but what he actually hated was his life. And although he was surrounded by competent professionals, none was trained to attend to the part of Brooks that was the most damaged: his spirit and his self-esteem.

The hospital may have called in a therapist or two, but Brooks could, in his language, "bullshit" them. He was not going to give in, to try to make things better: He was too mad. Starting with his wife, he had been chewing up and spitting out therapists for years. Now, he decided to be "beyond hope." He wasn't going to cooperate with the universe any more.

In spite of his discomfort, this time Brooks wasn't in imminent danger of dying, so I didn't feel panicked or terrified. I just felt sad for him. I also felt that, regardless of his condition, he would do better with a sane and happy wife, and I was rather fond of sanity and happiness myself. So I went to work, laughed, and tried to stay centered. Knowing that he was alone in the hospital, I felt guilty when, occasionally, I went out to dinner with friends or otherwise took time off, but at the same time I realized how important it was to take care of myself.

On that long-ago December night when Brooks first became ill, we had run a sprint to the finish line. After winning the race for his life, we abandoned the sprint for a marathon, and in the last few years, the pace had slowed to a comfortable trot. Now the rules of the race had changed again, but this time I was determined to compete at a pace that would allow me to breathe. I would be a support, a very strong support, but one who knew her limits and stayed within them. I had learned not to stretch too far, lest we both be stung by the snap-back.

I was curious, however, as to why he wasn't starving, since he had nothing good to say about the hospital's food, and it was clear he wasn't eating the food I brought him. When I asked him, he avoided answering. On one early-morning visit, I discovered the answer. Brooks had a "food fairy." More than that, he had a "Caribbean Angel."

In this large facility with rules, structures, and complex protocols, this kind, intuitive woman, who cleaned Brooks' room every morning, saw past the patient in the bed. Instead of a man who couldn't lift his head, a man who was angry at life and at all who loved him, she saw the handsome airline pilot who had been master of his world, and she loved his stories.

Brooks' angel came from a Caribbean nation where he had landed weekly during most of his commercial airline career. He knew the layout of the airport on her island and the route into the town where she had grown up and where her family still lived. Brooks had made a friend. She was captured in the wide net of his charm, his smile, and his twinkling eyes, and he had her convinced that she was the best Caribbean cook in the United States.

Brooks had used his charm to go fishing for food, and both the nourishment and nurture of his catch saved his life. Soon this hard-working mother, who had come to the States for a better life for herself and her kids, was going home at night and making Brooks' favorite Caribbean dishes. Each morning she brought them to the hospital, no doubt taking delight in watching him eat his big meal of the day as she was cleaning his room. The spice was in her food, but the warmth came from her heart.

It was not only Brooks who benefited from the understanding of this compassionate woman. She also helped me to see Brooks' power and to hold onto my own. The marathon may have begun again, but this time I wasn't in the race alone. Brooks had a lot of problems, *and* he had a lot of strengths, *and* he knew how to take care of himself. We were still contributing members of the same team, caring for each other but also able to care for ourselves, even in the worst of times.

• • •

After Brooks' surgery and rehab, the doctors thought they had been successful, and for a few months things seemed to stabilize. Then it became clear that he was getting worse.

By that time I had adjusted to Brooks' short-term

memory loss: I expected him to be confused sometimes, or to not remember things at all. Like a kid with ADD, or like any of us on occasion, he remembered those things that interested him most or those he considered important, often very different from the things I found important. If he had a good night's sleep, Brooks thought he had been sleeping well for weeks; if he slept poorly, he thought this, too, was the status quo.

So when he complained that his leg was worse, sadly for him, at first I didn't give his complaints much credence. I told him the doctors believed they had stopped the damage and that he would be okay. On this subject, however, Brooks was not confused. He *was* having trouble walking and standing, exhibiting that slowness of gait I had first seen in Spain.

Months later, I took him to a crusty, experienced neurologist at a famous hospital, a fellow who had been recommended as the doctor of last resort. This man reviewed the records from the dozens of other doctors we had visited, looked at films of Brooks' head and neck, and then laid out—better than anyone ever had before—the realities of Brooks' condition.

As we sat in his office, this doctor explained that any one of Brooks' problems would have been unlikely to result in such a significant and rapid decline in his functioning. But when you put all of his problems together, they conspired to create a kind of "perfect storm" that raged through his brain and spinal column, damaging the circuitry and blurring the messages that needed to flow through his body.

When Brooks left to use the restroom, this kind, straightforward professional pulled no punches. He told me that Brooks' condition was progressive. If he lived long enough, he could be paralyzed from the neck down, and in the meantime, an accident or fall could result in instant paralysis. He said there was no way to know how quickly Brooks would decline, but that he *would* decline. He told me to stop looking for answers, to move forward with our lives, and never to let anyone operate on Brooks' neck again. All that could be done, had been done.

When Brooks returned, this experienced doctor, who some found difficult to deal with but whom I appreciated for his intense study and honest words, got up from his desk, put his arm around Brooks, and told us to go home and enjoy our lives together.

I decided to keep the doctor's prognosis to myself. Intuitively, I knew he was correct, but I also knew that he wasn't God, and neither was I. There was no way to know how slowly or quickly Brooks' condition would change, and he didn't need the apparent inevitability of his fate thrown in his face. I didn't feel burdened by this secret. I tucked it away, drawing it out only when I needed help in understanding a new symptom or when we visited a doctor. At the same time, I knew it wasn't really a secret. Brooks lived in his body. He could feel what was happening. Still, he seemed more irritated than frightened by the changes he felt. His cognitive problems had given him some kind of grace, an acceptance he didn't have before his illness.

We had come to a crossroads. We could keep searching for answers that even I now believed would never come. We could wait anxiously for the worst to happen, wasting our "better" days in the process, or we could grab the life available to us, hold tightly to each other, and run until each of us, in our own way, could run no more.

Whether we talked about it or not, I knew my husband and knew what he would want if he thought he were in a steep decline, with only a few years left to walk or breathe. Brooks loved to travel: Along with flying airplanes, it was one of the reasons he became a pilot, a profession that even now afforded us many discounted travel opportunities. Thus the moment the physician told us the prognosis, I made a decision. Over the next several years, I was going to take advantage of as many of these opportunities as possible. New problems would eventually reveal themselves, but for now, we were going to play this baby out.

Later that week, I called friends in Paris.

CHAPTER 12
Opportunity

"In the middle of difficulty lies opportunity."
Albert Einstein

- For almost every opportunity, there are costs as well as benefits.

- When seeking or accepting the benefits, it is important to think about the price you are willing to pay, because it is impossible to avoid the costs.

- The fat checkbook brings new expectations, and the new shoe sometimes gives us a blister.

- Be ready, at any time, to renegotiate.

Paris, London, Vienna, California, Vancouver, Dallas, Chicago, Orlando, New York, Colorado, Phoenix, Edmonton, and other points on the globe

Here's what I learned:

- When others are simply strolling, you are getting a great workout by pushing a 220-pound man in a wheelchair.

- Join your husband in learning to love the smell of jet fuel early in the morning. Early flights usually leave on time and have fewer passengers.

- Do not wear a funky fake fur coat in the rain in New York City while you are trying to get a cab and your husband is in a wheelchair. No one will stop.

- It does not matter what you wear in the rain in Paris while trying to hail a cab. If your husband is in a wheelchair, no one will stop.

- If your husband is in a wheelchair and you are visiting your kids in the center of Vienna, strap him down. Many streets are cobblestone, and it will take him days to stop vibrating.

- Avoid Frankfurt Airport altogether.

- The Americans with Disabilities Act makes it much easier for the disabled to travel in this country. For the disabled and their caregivers, getting around in other countries is much more challenging.

- When a foreign hospital advertises they are "English-speaking," they are referring primarily to the doctors. If your husband has an emergency in the middle of the night and your knowledge of the native language is limited to the word "eggplant," look for a nurse from the Philippines. These hard-working women are all over the world, and most of them speak English.

- If a child throws up in the train that goes through the Chunnel from London to Paris and the wheelchair has been stowed for the trip, there is no escape and it is totally gross.

- You can only eat so much fondue.

- People are nice in every country, and as human beings, we are more alike than we are different. If you look for these similarities, you will make friends wherever you go.

- Do not listen to your husband, he of odd directions, when you are driving and he has discovered a "sure-fire" short-cut over the Alps.

- When possible, regardless of where you are, take the train with the glass dome.

- If you love the salmon in Seattle, don't bother to ship some home in order to recreate the experience unless you know what to do with it once it gets there.

- If you and your husband are on the carousel at Disney World and you see someone stealing his wheelchair, think twice before you decide to jump off and run after the thief. You could injure your ankle, and then no one in the family will be able to walk.

- There is a cool museum of Western art near Dallas/Fort Worth, but think before you agree that your husband should buy a lot of western posters. You could spend the rest of your life in a family room adorned by pictures of cowboys, horses, and train robberies, jockeying for space with the airplanes and bombs "bursting in air" that may be there already.

- Learn to love the West. You may end up with many kids and cute grandkids who prefer cowboy boots to bare feet in the sand.

- Never drive a car in Boston.

- When you are in an airport and you find a skycap to help with the wheelchair and your luggage, beg him to stay with you until you are in the car or on the train; then give him every cent you have.

- Be grateful for every opportunity.

- Do not expect help, but let others know how much you appreciate their kindness.

- When on a tour, do not let people, mostly nice men who feel uncomfortable seeing a woman hoisting a wheelchair, help you lift or push the chair all of the time. Eventually, they will feel responsible or even resentful. Don't take it personally. It's human nature, and they are on vacation, too.

- Do not expect to travel on Super Bowl Sunday, no matter where you are. Every European city has a Marine barracks that guards the embassy, and your husband will talk his way in to watch the game.

- Learn to say "Thank you," "Please," and " Excuse me" in every language. This will carry you far.

- You can survive more clear-air turbulence than you ever imagined.

- Get to know the housekeeping staff at every hotel, be very nice to them, and give them lots of money. When your husband falls they will try to help you, and their lives may be far more difficult than yours.

- When you have to leave your daughter in Eastern Europe with her newborn and you are helping her choose a babysitter, forget things like ideology and the politics of the country involved. Go for the warm, loving Communist every time.

- When at a big-city medical center waiting for your husband to have dozens of medical tests, there is almost always some inexpensive place to get your nails done.

- Do not allow your disabled husband, regardless of what he and his buddy believe, to go canoeing down an alligator-infested river. At some point he *will* be expected to walk and carry the canoe.

- Realize that, regardless of the political ideology of the country, all people want an opportunity to build a better life for themselves and their kids. So when you meet a person who used to be a high-level government official in the former Soviet Union, do not be shocked when she asks how to get her daughter into an American Ivy League university.

- Call your kids from wherever you are. The tables may have turned, and now they worry about you.

- Learn about Canadian prairie grass, elk, and moose. Your son may become a professor in those northern plains, produce two wonderful Canadian-American grandsons, and delight you with a daughter-in-law who teaches you a great deal about life.

- Do not let the wheelchair come between you and your husband. Choose to see the wheelchair as a tool, not a restriction.

- Go to bed early if you stay in a convent. They ring bells at 5 a.m.

- Understand that the world gets smaller daily. Do not be surprised when you walk into the apartment of a very nice woman who once worked for the East German government and you find IKEA furniture just like yours.

- Military cemeteries around the world are filled with brave men and women who fought so we could lead such privileged lives. Thank them, and thank their families.

- Love your life and all of the wonderful people who wish you well. Wish them well, too. We all are in this world together.

- Be grateful for your kids, learn to trust their judgment, and listen to your sons and daughters who both love and worry about you.

- Respect your kids' spouses and work to be lucky enough to include their parents among your best friends. Whenever possible, join together at every graduation, wedding, or birth. The joy of these extended family gatherings is more satisfying than any tour you will ever take.

- Keep your eye on your husband and know when the party is over.

- Go home.

- Cherish the small moments together. Understand, regardless of the challenges and changes, that if you are mindful enough to be generous with your love and appreciation, each stage of life is rich and meaningful.

- Don't be a hero. Allow yourself to receive the love that is given to you. Accept it with joy, and count your blessings.

- Try your best to savor every moment. Waste no time wanting something you cannot have. When you live in the moment that is available to you, you can build powerful and lasting memories that can help you endure any problem or challenge, memories that will cement the two of you together for the rest of time.

- And yes, "We'll always have Paris."

CHAPTER 13
Support

"The blessing lies next to the wound."
Author Unknown

Studies of Aging and Positive Attitude suggest....

- Human beings do better with support and a sense of purpose.

- In the paradoxical dance of humankind, one person's purpose often makes for another's support.

- We need support if we are to flourish, and when we accept this gift from another, it does not mean we are weak. In fact, our acceptance includes the gift of allowing the giver to have purpose.

- There is harmony to the music of our dance.

These last few years had taken us from early middle age to Grandma and Grandpa, and along the way there had been many changes in our lives, among them the fact that Brooks was doing great cognitively but could no longer walk unaided. Then Mia and Matt came back to the States from Europe, moving in with us while they looked for a house to meet the needs of their expanded family of four. After a few months, Matt and Mia suggested we settle together into an extended-family living situation. This arrangement would give these busy attorneys—Matt with an international organization whose job required travel, and Mia, a law professor at a university not far away—additional support as they built their careers. I would have support for Brooks when I was working, and Brooks, even when he didn't leave the house, would be surrounded by fun, activity, and purpose. The grandchildren, of course, would benefit from the love and care of all.

When the kids first suggested this arrangement, Brooks was delighted, but my joy was tempered by worry. It has always been important to me to be authentic with my kids about my feelings, without making them feel responsible for me. Knowing my daughter worried about Brooks and me, I was concerned about whether or not she felt responsible in some way for our well-being. I didn't want to mess up her marriage or her life, so I quizzed both her and Matt to make sure their suggestion of an extended-family home was as much about their needs and desires as ours, and they assured me this was true.

The picture of Matt, Mia, Brooks in his wheelchair with a grandchild on each knee, and me going up the wheelchair ramp of our new house, through the doorway, and into life as an extended family, is etched in my memory. To this day, as I watch my grandchildren reach each new milestone; as I see my grandson draw pictures of his family that include all of us, the two dogs, and the ramp leading to our door; and as I see my granddaughter place her grandfather's feet gently on the stirrups of his wheelchair, nonchalant about the fact that he cannot lift them himself, I know who benefits the most from this arrangement, and I am grateful. Our family life together has evolved into a comfortable and balanced arrangement, and we all work hard to make certain that everyone benefits.

I love our life with the kids, big and little, the joy of a spelling test aced, the bounce of a tennis ball against the garage door, or the familiar smell of Neatsfoot Oil rubbed on a glove when baseball season starts. I never imagined Brooks and I would live with our children, that he would be disabled, that things would change so much from when we first met, or that my life could have so many unplanned but wonderful dimensions.

Sometimes, on quiet mornings after the school bus has rolled away and Matt and Mia have gone off to their respective offices and Brooks is sleeping soundly in our bed, I take a few minutes to stroll through the flowering shrubs and stately trees surrounding our home. During those times I often think about life and about the unexpected benefits we so often find hidden among the obvious costs.

For instance...

Because of our wooded yard, which we all love but which sometimes attracts unwanted critters, we ended up with a house full of mice. The exterminator, answering our urgent call, put out a type of bait that makes mice thirsty. The idea, he explained, was for them to eat the bait, then run outside looking for water.

A few weeks later, I was awakened early one morning by Mia's screams of, "Mouse, mouse!" Her high-pitched shrieks coming from the direction of the kitchen shattered my sleep. Curious as to why this competent, solid woman would begin her day with such noise, I ran to the kitchen to find my take-charge, lawyer daughter acting as if she might have been a twelve-year-old. "There's a mouse in the sink," she gasped, drawing her hands and arms close to her body and raising her bare feet up off the floor until she was standing on her toes, as if surrounded by hundreds of mice. She reminded me of a picture in a well-read Cinderella storybook of long ago, where the soon-to-be princess is standing on tiptoe to avoid stepping on the coachmen, who have turned to mice at her feet.

Mia's seven-year-old son danced around the sink, all too eager to engage the mouse in some early-morning action, while her nine-year-old daughter's eyes filled with compassion for this poor little rodent, who in his quest for water had clearly taken a wrong turn.

Faced with this scenario, I did what any sane person

would do. I called in our Marine! To his credit, Brooks made his way from bed to wheelchair, over the ramps inside the house, and into the kitchen in record time. Looking at the mouse, a formidable creature of at least an inch in length, he said to our vibrating grandson, "Get me the baseball bat."

Opening the garage door and tossing sports equipment all over the floor, the seven-year-old recruit went in search of the perfect weapon. Meanwhile, our granddaughter began screaming, "No, no. I want to keep him for a pet."

As have many leaders preparing for war, Lt. Colonel Grandpa lied, assuring all of us that he planned to only "stun" the invader. Siding with her daughter, Mia pleaded for diplomacy and peace in the kitchen sink, as her son returned with a Louisville Slugger in hand.

Mia was about to plead for non-violence once again when she saw the clock and realized the kids were going to be late for school and she for work. Quickly, she turned her attention to the kids, hustling them away from the stainless steel war zone and to the bus stop at the top of the driveway.

Shortly thereafter, I followed this diverse political group up the driveway to the garbage can, carrying in my hand the opposing army of one, now quite still in a plastic storage bag.

My granddaughter asked if her potential pet would be okay, and I assured her he would be fine once he got over his "really big" headache. "He has a headache?" she hurled indignantly at me as she glared suspiciously at the bag and stepped onto the waiting bus.

The mouse was gone, and Mia, to her great relief, did not have to touch it. She made it to court on time, Brooks got to be a Marine, and the kids will have something to talk about in therapy when they are 30.

As I walked back to our kitchen, I laughed at this early morning exercise in cost-benefit ratios, realizing how well our extended family arrangement works for all of us (with the exception, of course, of the poor mouse with the unquenchable thirst, the bad directional system, and the really big headache).

CHAPTER 14
Closure

---

*"You cannot discover new oceans unless you have
the courage to lose sight of the shore."*
Anonymous

- Giving new meaning to difficult life events can help us to accept our situation, find closure, and move on with our lives.

- This cognitive reframe may lead us to great lessons and new growth.

- Growth does not come without risk.

Brooks' cerebral hemorrhage, which happened right after he returned from a ski racing camp with Andy and David, ended not only his career as a commercial airline pilot but also his ability to pursue his other love, skiing.

In the years immediately following his hemorrhage, doctors had told Brooks to avoid high altitudes because of reduced atmospheric pressure. Since the source of the bleeding in his brain had never been determined, the doctors were worried that exposure to reduced pressure might cause the vulnerable area to bleed again.

Now almost a decade later, Brooks had survived many different kinds of "stress tests" without harm, including exposure to higher altitudes. When it was time to travel, we both knew the drill, and we knew how to get help if we needed it. Even so, we had never discussed his feeling of loss at not being able to ski. In fact, Brooks wanting to ski wasn't even on my radar screen.

So, when Brooks started talking about how much he missed skiing, about the fact that this was the trip he *really* wanted to take, I was shocked. The idea of him skiing down a mountain seemed about as bad an idea as I could think of, so I did nothing to drive his dream forward. Regardless of his desires, I felt I had good reason for my reluctance, since his spinal cord problems are in his cervical collar (his neck), and I remembered the prognosis of that crusty neurologist at the famous hospital years before: An accident or fall could result in instant paralysis. I could only imagine how his physicians would react if they were consulted now.

One day, even though by this time he could take only one or two steps unaided and his mobility depended upon a wheelchair or electric scooter, he told me that he thought he could ski again. Compared with Brooks, I am not much of a risk-taker, and this time was no exception, so I gave him a hug, that kind that says, "I am so sorry for you." I should have known better. Brooks was serious. He was *not* going to be the object of my pity nor the victim of my reluctance.

Brooks was on a campaign. As his ability to walk had declined, he had fought using a cane, a walker, a wheelchair, or a scooter, resisting at every juncture until he'd had no choice. Now he was trying to see his wheelchair as a tool, but in many ways it still felt like a restriction, and I think this is why skiing one more time became so important. It was a way to assert his independence, to say to himself, *I am still me.*

I also believe there was another reason. Brooks was born to ski. He had first learned this sport in college. In fact, it was skiing that led to his short-lived occupational detour as a taxi driver in Aspen, and although neither skiing nor taxi driving was to become his profession, skiing *was* to become his avocation.

• • •

Before his hemorrhage, Brooks was captain of his airline's ski team. He also was involved in the formation of a ski federation that brought together the members of other airline ski teams for competitive races four times each winter. They flew the flags of their airlines as, terrific athletes all, they sped downhill on steep, rutted slalom courses, vying for championship medals for themselves and their teams.

These week-long competitions included men's racing teams, women's teams, family ski time, and great nightly parties. For a fairly conservative girl from rural Ohio, these were some of the wildest parties I had ever seen. It wasn't that anything all that crazy happened, but these parties were the hottest ticket in town, often frequented by famous skiers and celebrities looking for a good time. There was one big reason these parties were so popular: the presence of the flight attendants.

In those years most pilots were men, so the bulk of the women ski-team members were flight attendants. I was fairly intimidated when I first joined Brooks on these outings, since these women were not only gorgeous, they were also skilled athletes. I, on the other hand, was terrified of skiing, and while I am okay to look at, I have always been a little round: You would never mistake me for a lean and willowy flight attendant.

What I soon learned is that these flight attendants were hard-working women, just like me. Many of them had children, went to school on the days they were not working, and needed to be in shape so they could open heavy doors and do what needed to be done to protect their passengers. Safety was their number-one priority. It didn't take long for my intimidation to turn to admiration for these women, for their athletic skills, their brains, and often for their beauty. There was a lot I was to learn from them.

Before I met Brooks, I had gone skiing only once in my life. One look at the steep stretch in front of me evoked catastrophic thoughts of death and destruction, and arousal hormones poured through my body, sending me into a panic attack. I was so terrified that I made the chairlift operator take me down the hill as well as up. Now I was with this guy who thought skiing was as natural as breathing and who was confident that I could both catch on and catch up without difficulty.

My first problem was that I had no ski clothes and didn't know what I needed. For that matter, I had no skis. Some flight attendants came to my rescue, took me shopping, and along the way, pointed out the best place to get skis sharpened so they would be faster. (Trust me, I had no desire to sharpen my skies.) One woman even showed me the best location for a soothing après ski soak in a hot tub. Oh sure, like I'm going to sit in a hot tub with a bunch of gorgeous women. At that time in my life, I had enough problems with my self-confidence. The last thing I needed to do was to appear in a bathing suit, too.

Even so, it was fun for me to be in this setting. I love to work, and to this day I am excited when I walk into my office. Left to my own devices, I mostly work. These ski camp weeks were filled with people who both worked hard and played hard, and they helped me to understand that as much as you might love your profession or your family, there is a value to stepping away from responsibility and just blowing off some steam. So, while I didn't follow all the advice I was given, I did buy some ski clothes.

Brooks' confidence in my ability to learn to ski and his determination that I join him for those ski adventures forced me to risk more than I wanted, to stretch more than I thought possible, and, in the process, to learn more about myself. All I had to do was to conquer the sport, along with my terror at the *thought* of learning to conquer the sport. For years I'd been telling clients about the cognitive behavioral principle that our thoughts affect our feelings and our feelings affect our behavior. Now I had a chance to prove it.

I hate speed, and at that time I had never been to the top of such big mountains. I grew up in Ohio; it was flat. And while I agreed there was much to be said for a snow-covered landscape, the truth is, I preferred dirt. Actually, I liked black dirt, with its accompanying smell of clover and organic fertilizer when it drifted across a field of clover on a summer day. Standing at the top of a mountain and looking down on a forbidding landscape of white was as foreign to me as arriving in Ohio must have been for my European ancestors.

And as for speed, it may seem odd that someone comfortable with a much more measured pace would choose to marry a pilot who could do loops in fast little jets, fly hundreds of miles an hour across the country, and traverse a ski slope at what seemed to be the speed of light. But, of course, this was one reason I was attracted to Brooks. He knew things I didn't know, and he encouraged me to go places I hadn't been, both figuratively and literally.

I have read in business books that confidence is no more than the personal appraisal of one's own potential. Since I had no vision of my potential as a skier, I learned to ski by leaning on Brooks' confidence, though I wouldn't say he was the most loving or patient teacher. He basically told me I was a good athlete and that my problems with skiing were all "in my head," and he demanded I join him on cold and snowy mornings when the lifts opened. I would like to tell you that Brooks spent all of his time skiing with me, but the truth is, he usually told me to go sign up for a morning class while he went off to race with the guys. Not knowing what else to do, I dutifully signed up for class after class after class. During the first few classes, I was the worst student. In time I made it into the bottom third of the class, an improvement, but a poorer performance than I had ever put forth in twelve years of public school, four years of college, or four years of graduate school. I did not like this situation.

After class I would meet Brooks for lunch and then show him my new and progressing abilities. Our skill levels were so far apart, however, that he was rarely impressed, and neither was I. If I whined enough, he would pull himself away from the better skiers and spend afternoons on the slopes with me, but being with me was tedious for him, I am sure.

After awhile, I came to agree with Brooks that my problems with skiing were "mostly in my head," and later still I stopped the classes altogether. It was not the technical understanding of skiing that was my problem, although it is a well-known fact that anxiety inhibits learning. Clearly, most of my problems on the slopes had to do with my negative thoughts, my belief in my impending death by snow, and my anger at myself for allowing these thoughts to continue. I was caught in a vicious cycle, because the more catastrophic thinking I did, the worse I skied, and the worse I skied, the more I was ticked off at my poor performance. I wanted to live, but I also wanted to succeed. Remember, I am a striver and Brooks is a glider. To realize the potential within me, I needed to change my thinking, relax, and stop worrying.

So for many years I trudged out West with Brooks, forcing myself to hop on a ski lift, trying to figure out how to conquer both the sport and myself. In time I invited my old friends, Tom and Carol, to join us for race weeks, and when Tom went off to ski with Brooks and the guys, Carol and I worked on our skiing together. We laughed, we took rests, and we chose the easy courses. One day, with my smiling face warmed by the sun and my hands warmed by waterproof snow mittens, with my ski poles firmly in hand and my knees bent in the proper position for each turn, I had a breakthrough.

By this time I had conquered much of my fear and no longer saw death or destruction at the bottom of the course.

I knew that when I relaxed and just had fun I could ski as well as Carol and actually as well as many of the other women at race week. But that was not the point. What happened on that sun-drenched, snowy peak is that I came to terms with the fact that skiing was not my strength, that I would never be a racer, and that, best of all, I didn't need to be a racer. I just needed to glide.

When I got back to the top of the hill, I accepted myself for who I was. When I stopped dwelling solely on my inadequacies, I was able to draw from the strength of the mountains surrounding me. I reached out to those mountains and to the glistening, snow-packed course in front of me, marveled at the beauty of the aspens that lined the edges of the path, and had the best ski run of my life. I felt free of both my fear and my striving.

I will never be much more than a really low intermediate skier, but from that day on, I kept my fear in check and led with my courage. That is the lesson I learned from Brooks' persistence.

• • •

Brooks' passion for skiing began in his college days. Family legend has it that Brooks' dad, who had only an eighth-grade education but was a luggage buyer for a big Midwestern department store, took his negotiating expertise with him as he peddled his son's academic, athletic, and leadership skills to many colleges. Things were different back then, and the story goes that one prestigious college went for the deal and offered Brooks a scholarship and his dad a payment plan.

But Brooks wanted no part of it. His dad's deal would have sent him east, and Brooks, a cowboy even then, wanted to go west, with Stanford as his goal. When his mom learned that the negotiated plan did not match Brooks' dream, she intervened, and his dad scrimped and saved to send his first-born son to the college of his choice.

After educating our six kids, Brooks still feels a little guilty about not taking the offer his dad negotiated. But it was because of Stanford that he learned to ski.

Many of Brooks' college friends came from wealthy families with vacation homes, and because they were his buddies, he was often invited to join them when they headed for the snowy peaks and the deep powder of the slopes. In those years he had no ski clothes, so he skied in his jeans, but from his first moment on the slopes, headed at top speed toward the sun, he says he knew he had come home to a sport that would be with him for the rest of his life.

This love of skiing never abated. Brooks taught his three kids to ski soon after they learned to walk. He took them to airline ski weeks, taught them to race, and helped them develop into great skiers. On his days off he even found a little icy bump near his home where he became a ski coach for other kids, teaching them to race toward their futures.

When I met Brooks, it was not just me that he was set on introducing to the sport. He was also tenacious in his determination that my kids learn to ski, and, as he did with his own kids, he spent hours on the hills helping them to build proficiency. Because of Brooks, JC and Mia became pretty good skiers, and Andy became an excellent one.

In fact, we used to joke that when either David or Andy skied down a mountain, they both had exactly the same movements and style as Brooks. I could understand that of David, Brooks' son, but it was nurture, not nature, that made Andy such a proficient skier. Matthew, also a great skier, spent part of his high school years at a ski school in Vermont, and it was a proud day for Brooks when we stood on the side of a hill and watched him compete in the state skiing championships. And because of Brooks, both Matthew and Andy succeeded in making it to the Junior Olympics.

Brooks, in his own quiet and competent way, is an expansive man. Because of his passion for skiing, he gave his kids and mine both a love of the mountains and the skills to enjoy them, with the result that five of our six kids live in western climates. In fact, I remember the time when Andy was a junior in high school and I took him to look at colleges in the West. David came too, since he was only a couple of years younger and wanted to follow in the same direction. I remember sitting in the Denver airport and watching with pride as the two boys pored over books that described each college in detail. I imagined they were look-ing at student-teacher ratios, the number of doctoral-level professors in each department, or the percentage of each school's graduates that continue on to graduate school. However, Brooks had taught his lessons well, and what they were actually doing was estimating which college was nearest the most vertical drop—in other words, which school would give them the best access to skiing!

.   .   .

When Brooks began his campaign to hit the slopes again, he was even willing to consider a program for disabled skiers. These programs, run by teams of heroes who volunteer their time to assist the disabled, outfit each skier with outriggers (crutch-like devices with small skis at the end) to help with stability. Recognizing Brooks' determination, I decided it was time to make clear the possible consequences of a fall so that he could fully evaluate the cost-benefit ratio of his decision. So I explained the risks, tried to make certain he understood them, and then worked to persuade him that skiing was just too risky a proposition. Despite the risks, Brooks was confident that he could take a few runs without falling. The truth was, in my gut (but not in my head), I kind of agreed.

Taking a deep breath and pinning my coattails to his confidence, I acquiesced, checked out which ski resorts had programs for disabled skiers, and waited as long as Brooks would allow before actually making any real plans. After Mia and Matt agreed to join us, I called the rest of the kids to tell them we were heading west. "Grab your skis," I said, "Grandpa wants one last run."

We landed in Denver, staying with Andy and his new wife Meaghan for a day or two so that Brooks could adjust to the altitude slowly. (Fortunately, Andy and Meaghan had just bought their first home in the area, and this one didn't have a keg room.) Meanwhile, the other kids and the first three of what have now become nine grandchildren arrived, and our caravan took off to Breckenridge, a ski resort about two hours from Denver.

When we reached our destination, the sun glistened off the packed snow that covered the well-groomed ski runs. As I looked up the hill from the parking lot, I remembered all of the times we had made this trip in years past. This time, with the boys pushing Brooks in his wheelchair and three grandkids bursting with excitement at going to ski school, we headed to the hut housing the skiers who volunteer their time to help the disabled feel the rush and beauty of skiing.

Once we reached the hut, the little kids went off to their lessons and the adults crowded around as Brooks learned how to use the outriggers that would help him stay upright and stable on the snow. Eventually, all of us headed to the chairlift, with the disabled-skiing coaches pushing Brooks in his wheelchair through snow and over ice—not an easy task. When it came time for Brooks to get on the chairlift, the operator stopped it from moving, and with the help of his ski guides, he was loaded onto the seat. One volunteer sat with him, and I took a seat on the chair behind them.

When we reached the top, the chairlift stopped again so that Brooks, with the help of his volunteer guides, could get off, grab his outriggers, and gain stability on the packed snow that was once again beneath his feet.

I worried as we went up the mountain, remembering the time a chairlift had stopped working with Andy on board and how he had been stranded high in the air, swinging in the cold mountain breeze for over two hours. Actually, I was worrying about so many things on that ride that I totally forgot that I hadn't skied in almost a decade.

When it was my turn to step off the lift and ski away from the chair, I lost my balance, crossed my skies and fell flat on my face. When the guys who were there to help Brooks saw me fall, they left his side and came to mine.

Since at that moment I had done a face plant, I never saw the twinkle in Brooks' eyes, which in any case was probably hidden behind the helmet he was wearing to protect his head. But I know it was there as Brooks, seizing the moment, pointed both his skis and his outriggers straight down the mountain and took off.

When his skiing guides saw the back of his bright yellow, red, and turquoise ski jacket speeding away, with his skis pointed directly toward the bottom of the hill, they panicked and took off after him. This crew was followed quickly by our kids, who, because they knew of Brooks' strength, were not surprised when they saw that in an apparent attempt to stay balanced, he was using his outriggers but had somehow lifted his "bad" leg (the one that will not support his weight) slightly above the snow. Brooks was not just skiing straight down the mountain, he was doing it on one leg!

I watched Brooks lead this parade until they were out of sight. Then I carefully got situated on my skis, pushed off, made my little turns, and skied from one side of the slope to the other, taking what seemed like three hours, until I reached the group assembled around Brooks at the bottom of the hill.

Only half in jest, I called him a jerk and was reminded of all those other times when Brooks took me on ski runs that terrified me and put me in situations I thought I couldn't handle. (In fact, there is a famous story among our friends who, passing overhead on a chairlift, overheard me call Brooks a really bad name for believing I could master such a scary course.)

However, when I called him a jerk on this day, I was also laughing, reminded of the feeling of freedom that Brooks helped me to learn to appreciate as the wind and snow blew into my face. I thought of how he had taught me to use all of my strength, to set my own course, and to be determined in my pursuit of mastering the lessons I needed to learn.

Brooks made other, more gentle runs down the mountain that day. He behaved, and his guides were in awe of both his power and his skill. The kids took off in many directions, and the grandkids learned to "make a pizza" with their skies so they could stop, and to make two "hot dogs" when they wanted to go straight.

Late afternoon began to creep into the day, as it had into our lives, and soon the lowering sun brought a chill to the air and along with it, a message. Brooks, now quite tired, with both legs beginning to fail and most of his weight on the outriggers, took one final, easy run down the mountain with me and the guides. When we reached the bottom, we both knew this was the last time Brooks would ever be on skis. But this time, *he* was making the choice for it to be the last time. He had the closure that had eluded him since his hemorrhage, he had taken ownership of his life, and to the best of his ability, he was living life on his terms.

Brooks took off his helmet, turned to me and said, "Thank you."

"My pleasure," I lied.

Many would say that listening to my gut and supporting Brooks' desire to go skiing was questionable judgment, and I would agree. A few would say that listening to my head and not supporting his dream would have been questionable judgment, and I would agree. Sometimes you've just got to take the risk. Brooks was back.

CHAPTER 15
Resilience

"Whoever said, 'It doesn't matter whether you win or lose,' probably lost."
Martina Navratilova

- We are one unit: mind and body. Our leg moves, but the brain sends it the message to do so.

- Moving our muscles during exercise completes a complicated mind-body loop that results in chemical changes to our brain, affecting our mood, thoughts, and—through resultant changes in behavior—our lives.

- Without exercise, our muscles lose their tone and eventually their ability to move; the message is delivered but returned unopened.

- We are one unit with dual "controls," both mind and body, and each connects to the path that leads to our innate resilience, our ability to bounce back from adversity.

In my early twenties, long before I met Brooks, I fell in love with the beauty and power of tennis. The surge of strength and power that comes from hitting the ball squarely on the "sweet spot" of the racquet is a mirror to the grace and empowerment I feel from playing this game.

I am a thinker. I calculate risks, look at options, and understand cost-benefit ratios, but when faced with life's big decisions, it is my feet that guide me. The running, jumping, and vigorous exercise of tennis allow my mind and body to connect, leading me to my power, my resilience, and my future.

On a perfectly cool yet sunny day, standing on the backhand side of the grainy clay court while playing a league match for the local club, I had my first tennis epiphany. It was in this moment, as the upward spin of the tennis ball gave rise to *my* strength and power, that I finally gave myself permission to accept my feelings and make a decision I knew would ultimately change the future for myself and my kids. Some might have thought this decision hasty, but they didn't know that it's on the tennis court, with my mind and body working together, that I do my clearest thinking.

Tennis Epiphany #1: It is always true that when I use both my brain and my body, I find the clarity and strength to accept the choices I know are available to me and that will lead me forward to my future.

Some people talk about clearing their minds when they exercise, but I go one step further. When the mundane, everyday thoughts are cleared, it's as if I've made room for the bigger ideas, the questions for which there are no clear answers. It's almost like the back of my brain starts to percolate, and little bubbles of semiconscious thought, more pictures than words, begin some kind of instinctual processing. As I pound away at the ball, supercharging the feedback loops that connect brain and body, I have an awareness of both the bubbling thoughts and the tennis match itself. This feels good.

I love the blast of adrenaline that surges through my body when an opponent tries to intimidate me on the court. I enjoy the challenge and do my best to show them who is in charge (Bubble-Bubble/Power-Power).

When I succeed after lunging for a difficult return, I take joy in my execution. When these great moments elude me, I reaffirm my competence and prepare for the next shot, realizing that every action moves me forward and is a chance to learn (Bubble-Bubble/Confidence-Confidence).

When my practiced eye shows me an opponent's strengths and weaknesses, I adjust my game to incorporate this knowledge, using it to *my* advantage and to enhance *my* talents (Bubble-Bubble/Strength-Strength).

I love tennis more than almost anything in the world, and it is on the tennis court where I feel most in harmony with myself and the world around me. I may have asked Brooks, in years past, if he loved me as much as skiing or tennis, but he had the good sense not to ask me the same question. The game has been my reliable companion for years, and its effects provide a strong filament of resilience when times are tough.

Exercise is the world's best stress reliever. It increases the body's level of serotonin. It causes us to produce beta-endorphins, which give us a little "high," relieve pain, and make us want to exercise more. And, through a complex process, it protects us from long-term damage due to over-exposure to stress hormones. Our bodies are hard-wired for health and resilience. But long before I understood the biology of exercise, I felt it.

* * *

The first date I had with Brooks, the one after the softball game, was to play tennis. Our first arguments were about tennis, and it was on the court where I had my second tennis epiphany.

I am a "verbal" woman, and you might not want to have an argument with me. I like to think I can be both rational *and* verbal, but when Brooks and I were first together, it was hard to get him to "talk it out" if we were having an argument. Our communication on the tennis court was a little different. Brooks was a great player, and though he cut me a little slack, it was not enough, and I would leave the court feeling sullen and angry at my poor performance. I had a love-hate relationship about playing tennis with Brooks, and he had the same about arguing with me.

During our tennis-playing years, Martina Navratilova

and Jimmy Connors played an exhibition match. To compensate for the differences in their strength, she was given an *advantage*: He hit to the doubles line and she hit to the singles. After seeing that match, I decided that if Martina, whom I adored, could get past herself in this regard, then just maybe I could do the same. I suggested that Brooks and I play using these rules, thus giving me an advantage.

He readily agreed, and the next time we played I had a great time! Once again I felt competent, loved the game, and scored more than a few points. When the match was over, I left the court laughing, pleased we had connected both through our power and our love. (Brooks especially liked the part where I stopped spitting nails, since he was correct in assuming they eventually would have found their way through his skin and into his heart.)

Then it came to me!

Tennis Epiphany #2: The frustration I felt when I couldn't score a point, or even execute an expert stroke, when we played tennis under the old rules, must be similar to how Brooks felt when he tried to come up with words to counter my quick volleys during arguments. No wonder he didn't want to speak. This dynamic did not cater to his strengths. When we were having an argument, I needed to follow the new rules: I needed to give him an *advantage* by slowing down, talking less, and listening more.

Years later, when Brooks could no longer play tennis, I foolishly stopped playing, too. I was afraid of tipping the new, delicate balance of our relationship in either direction.

This went on for several years, and while I found other forms of exercise, nothing empowered and supported me like tennis.

One day, no longer an extension of Brooks, but weighed down by the platform of support I provided to him, I thought to myself, *This has got to stop. I need to play tennis. I miss my friend, my platform of support, the one that holds up both of us.*

Settled into our new extended family home, and with a feeling of closure from knowing that Brooks was functioning at an extremely high level, I decided it was time for me to return to the court. But it was not an easy start.

I felt both sad and guilty leaving Brooks at home when I went to play, so I signed up for a Friday-night round-robin and made dinner plans for after the match with another tennis-playing couple. That way, Brooks would go to the courts with me and watch the match; then we would join friends for dinner. I hoped this scenario would help Brooks feel as if he were a part of the action.

However, he resisted my attempts to keep him involved with the game, since the pain of his losses were so great. Each Friday that I played, he scowled at me from the sidelines, and at dinner afterward, he barely spoke to our friends. I was in a pickle. I didn't want to leave Brooks behind, but at the same time I didn't want to quit the game, which was sending fire and energy through my body.

Then I read about a group of guys who played wheelchair tennis, and I suggested we go to one of their camps so

Brooks could learn to use a chair to maneuver where his legs would not. Being a proud, all-or-nothing kind of guy, he refused.

Refusing to quit the game or allow him out of our Friday-night tennis dates, I made it very clear that wheelchair tennis camp was the only way out of his misery. This wasn't the time for balance, which, like a teeter-totter, would have left us suspended in midair. This was the time for a full frontal assault. Thus began the battle that eventually led to tennis epiphany number three.

Both Brooks and I are tough, determined people when we put our minds to it, so the pressure built and we were soon at war. It was a war I knew I had to win: My survival depended on the outcome, and in a paradoxical way, so did his. I also believed by now that wheelchair tennis would be great for Brooks, for reasons other than my own guilt and desire.

In spite of the pressure, this stubborn and powerful man continued to refuse my efforts, but my natural resilience had turned my determination to steel. After what seemed like an interminable number of Fridays, on a cool, clear night in autumn with a soft breeze floating across the court, Brooks finally caved. That night I had played a tough match and approached him with the joy of victory in my body language. Brooks, unable to take anymore and mustering all the dignity he could find, screamed at me with as much rage as consent, "Where is that goddamned wheelchair tennis camp you keep talking about? Find out where it is and let's go."

And so we did.

We headed to Cincinnati, where I witnessed some of the most incredible athletes imaginable. They were paraplegic, quadriplegic, had all kinds of physical challenges, and yet they never complained. They were amazing players (better than I ever could hope to be), and they filled the courts with strength, joy, laughter, determination, and competence. Brooks was older than the rest, but he quickly learned to use his chair in place of the legs that no longer supported him, and he soon recovered his tremendous tennis strokes. No longer needing to lean as much on me, Brooks began his roll to victory.

The rest was easy.

We got him a special wheelchair for tennis—red, with cantilevered wheels so it wouldn't tip. He worked hard learning to use it. Now he joins me on the court, plays with our local pro, and is right in the middle of the action when the family comes together for our annual day of tennis. Last year, Brooks and I played together in the Friday-night round-robin, and at dinner he regaled our friends with his great wheelchair tennis stories.

Tennis Epiphany #3: We cannot effectively take care of someone else unless we take care of ourselves, and, in taking care of another, we are, in a way unique to each of us, also taking care of ourselves.

For the next couple of years, I played tennis without guilt, sometimes as often as six times a week. I also played the best tennis of my life. Pushing a 220-pound man in a wheelchair up and down hills had built up not only my emotional strength, but my physical strength as well. I went from being a fairly powerful player to being a "power hitter," able to out-hit most women and many men. I walked like a jock, felt like a jock, and owned my power. I soon noticed the bubbles churning in the back of my brain again.

From the beginning of Brooks' medical problems, I had made the choice to keep my professional life within certain limits. This way I had time to care for him, care for our four parents who had died during the last decade, and be there for the kids, who could use a mother or grandmother from time to time. Now I had room for a new adventure.

I am an ambitious woman by nature. I like to learn, I like to teach, and I like to set and reach personal and professional goals. For the first time since those early December days, I felt as if my power had returned full force. I was beginning to own myself again, and I came to understand it was time to complete this reclamation effort, to go in the direction that, as if by a magnet, I am always pulled: forward.

I played, my brain bubbled. I played more—churn, bubble, churn. Tennis was leading me someplace, but I could see only faint glimmers of where that might be. Eventually, I saw an advertisement for a doubles tournament and begged Mia to play in it with me. When my wise and all-knowing daughter agreed, I knew, without her saying so, that she was doing it mostly for me.

I think of myself as a B to B+ player, and Mia as an A–

player. She was the captain of her high school tennis team, is even more powerful than I with her strokes, and has a wicked forearm. Although we made it to the finals of our division in a tournament won only once in history by a mother-daughter team, we were losing. Our opponents had managed to get us to play *their* game. Their choice of shots did not reveal our strengths, and we were playing (and losing) on their terms. My bruised ego led to tennis epiphany number four.

Mia and I had a quick powwow. If we were "going down," we decided, we would do it on our terms. If we were to lose, we would do it using our strengths and our best shots. So we plotted, and I set up her great forehand with a powerful, deep shot to my opponent's backhand side. The return was weak, and Mia, using all of her power, whaled the ball about a mile down the road.

"That's fine," I said, not wanting to tamper with the confidence I knew accompanied that power. "Keep it up. Hit the ball on your terms." The next forehand landed about 1000 feet down the road, the next 500, but within a couple of points, she landed one squarely in the court, a shot with such power that it could not be returned. Yes!

Point by point, we played our game, using *our* strengths, *our* skills, and *our* power, all of it compounded by the confidence that swirled through our veins. The crowd, feeling the energy, left other matches and moved to our court, intuitively understanding that something powerful was happening.

Point by point, we attacked until we owned the court. Our opponents were forced to fight against our strengths and to play *our* game, one they did not win. Finally we defeated our opponents and, with my determination intertwined with my daughter's supportive hand, we raised the trophy high. At 58 years old, and for the first time in my life, I became a tennis champion.

In his red tennis wheelchair with the cantilevered wheels, his well-worn racquet resting on his knees, Brooks cheered from the sidelines.

Tennis Epiphany #4: Do what you love, own your power, use your strengths, and no matter what, don't give up. This is where your true happiness will lie and where you will find the person you were born to be.

After the tournament, my brain was overflowing with bubbles, and I was ready to take the next big risk of my life, the risk of allowing myself to move forward by coming fully back to myself. Most of my life I had been lucky enough to follow my dreams, seize opportunity, and use my strengths. Now I was ready to take those dreams one step further, look for new opportunity, and use my strengths at another level. Tennis had taught me the power of doing what you love and that going forward did not mean I must leave others behind.

A few months later it was Christmas again, now more than a decade since that time when life for Brooks dimmed and nearly extinguished. On this Christmas night, with the path lit for me by my natural resilience and further brightened by the laughter of my children, my "bubbles" moved from feelings to words. My anniversary response revealed not sadness, but the excitement of my deepest dreams and desires.

I wanted to see if I could become a speaker and educator once again, reaching goals long ago left behind amid the responsibilities of life. I wanted to see if I could make it on the national stage. But this time, decades after my high-school and college speaking successes and those of my early years as an educator and clinician, my basket of life experiences was well-weathered, re-woven several times over, and overflowing with both professional *and* personal experience. Like the millions of tennis balls I had hit over the years, I had bounced back and was on the rise.

CHAPTER 16
Authenticity

"It is never too late to be what you might have been."
George Elliott

- Nature has set us up to succeed by being who we are.

- You are stronger than you think.

- Your innate resilience, personal power, and unique strengths can help you turn adversity into advantage.

I really didn't know how to approach becoming a national speaker or educator. I rarely watched professional speakers, and I had no clue how to act on my dreams. Finally, I thought of a friend, now deceased, who had told me years before that his wife, whom I had never met, was a speakers' agent. I went to the phone book, found where this woman now lived, and, having no computer skills, wrote her a letter in longhand.

For the first time, I voiced my goals to a complete stranger, and in ink. I told her of my personal and professional background, of my desire to talk about resilience and leadership, and that I wanted to be a top national speaker. I learned later that her surprise at my chutzpah was exceeded only by her shock at getting a *handwritten* letter. To her credit, she phoned to say she didn't know yet if she would represent me, but that I should rent a hall, invite an audience, tape my talk, and send her a copy.

And so I did.

I rented a room normally used for casual weddings, located not far from the tennis courts where I played. Then I pleaded with tennis buddies and neighbors to lay down racquets and obligations long enough to attend my 45-minute talk, promising them cookies and punch if they made it to the end. Lastly, I hired a wedding photographer to tape me (because I didn't know how to hire any other kind), explaining the situation to him when he arrived looking for the bride and groom.

I sent the agent the raw footage of this talk, and a week

later she called to say she was on board. We both knew I had a lot to learn.

Soon, I started speaking on a regular basis to any group that would have me, and often these groups required some convincing. If I thought the crowd would be thin, I begged friends to pack the room, and they came through time and again. Some would give me honest appraisals, while others just told me I was great. I needed both kinds of support, but all agreed they liked the question and answer period best, when I was relaxed and funny, more like me. It took me awhile to understand the significance of their comments.

While it may seem corny to others, I believe what I say. I use the principles I teach in my own life, and would not be here today if I didn't understand how to enhance the flexible platform of resilience that nature has programmed into each of us, or how to apply the skills and strategies I talk about to my own situation. And I would have stumbled long ago if I had not listened to my feelings, followed my dreams, and used my strengths to find the type of life and leadership that is authentic to me.

I believed my message even before I took it on the road, but in my first presentations, I tried too hard. I was teaching in a way that was too professorial, one that didn't show my love of fun as well as learning.

Driving to a talk one gray, October morning, I thought about the previous night's presentation. Everyone else seemed to think it was great, but I'd been disappointed. It didn't live up to my expectations, and I finally understood what my friends had been trying to tell me. I didn't get to laugh enough, didn't have fun, and was afraid to link content with the humor of real life, until, that is, I got to the unscripted questions. Then I relaxed and answered in a way that was more *me*, and the audience knew it.

That morning, while stopped at a red light with both hands firmly grasping both the steering wheel and my future, I decided to quit worrying about being so perfect, go with my strengths as an educator, and just have fun.

I have spent decades studying resilience and human behavior, and I have a lot of scientific knowledge. But I am also a daughter, stepdaughter, wife, former wife, mother, stepmother, mother-in-law, grandmother, businesswoman, caregiver, and leader. I understand, because I've lived it, how we can learn and grow in ways that enhance our natural resilience, and how this growth can lead us to an authentic style of leadership and to a better life. I also know that many people have lives far more difficult than mine. While every situation is different, I understand from my own life, and from what others have taught me, what it's like to be a working woman whose family depends on her for both the purchase and preparation of nourishment and the warm embrace of nurture. I get it.

The study of Positive Psychology teaches us that having a purpose in life, combined with using our strengths, will lead to our true happiness. Finally, the light bulb went on, and I realized it's true: Like everyone else, the best gift I have to offer others is me. I know I am not perfect and that my challenges are not as severe as those faced by many people, but I have come to discover that my greatest strength lies in my willingness to accept who I am, follow my passions, and focus on what is right, rather than what is wrong, with me and with others.

Life is not always pretty, and there is much to be learned—not only from the sunny days or the rainbows, but also from the dark days, the hours of gloom and sorrow, and the black grip of fear.

The fact is, nothing is forever, everything changes, we can't control the world, balance only lasts for the moment, and it is all okay. We are made to survive; we just have to individualize the details. My details are not your details, but the principles of resilience, strength, and authentic leadership remain the same.

Our greatest survival strategies are already within us; it's just a matter of digging down and pulling them out. But we don't have to do it alone. Sometimes we develop problems such as anxiety or depression. These are not mental problems. Rather, these are problems with biological, psychological, and environmental components that affect our mood and sometimes our ability to function. But it's a new world, and effective help is available. Reaching out for help doesn't mean that we're weak or we should be embarrassed. Reaching out gets us centered again, allowing us to approach the world with all the strengths within us.

One of those strengths is our innate resilience. What is the sense of being hard-wired to overcome adversity if we never have tough times? Having it good all the time doesn't take us anywhere; we don't learn anything. When we have tough times, at home or at work, we develop confidence, strength, and, eventually, our authentic leadership style. It's what we are *meant* to do.

I am grounded firmly in the belief that we are defined, not by what happens to us in life, but by the choices we make in response to life's events. Should I forget this fact, I need only look at my husband, the face of courage, to whom I owe a great debt for all he has taught me through his love, expectations, and determination. Or I can turn to the women and men I have met throughout the years, who, by enhancing their resilience and defining their own strengths, are leading their families, companies, country, and the world into this infant century.

I know how lucky I am to have such a life; I am grateful for the privilege and hope I don't blow the opportunity.

I believe in hope, and on that gray, damp October morning I hit my stride. When the traffic light turned green and I turned the corner, it was a directional change that would take me to the next chapter of my life, to the stages of convention centers, corporations, and other venues around the world.

I soon discovered, however, that turning the corner was just a beginning, that my desire for new adventures had propelled me into an entirely new universe. I have read that top performers often demonstrate the self confidence to see themselves as more talented than others might believe them to be. When I walked onto the stage to deliver my first keynote address to hundreds of people, after spending a year or so doing smaller breakout sessions, I understood why this was so.

The performer in me loves the connection with the audience, but when I walked on stage that night, there was nothing in front of me but an ocean of darkness. The faces of the audience were obscured by the brightness of the lights surrounding me, and I felt more alone under those spotlights than I ever had on a snowy mountain peak. I started to sweat, my heart rate was off the charts, with my breathing beginning to match it, and I was getting dizzy. As the first few words came from my mouth, I thought, *What have I done?*

I'd loved doing the break-out sessions, having an opportunity to talk in depth about topics such as resilience, leadership, and the mind-body connection, but I'd continued to have my eye on doing a keynote address. In the speaking world, the keynoter is the Big Kahuna. Now I'd made it, but I was staring at a faceless audience, knowing they were staring back at me, and I thought I was going to barf. I was speaking so fast that if I kept it up, I would deliver the entire forty-five minute presentation in about ten minutes. To make matters worse, I had two dialogues going at once: the one the audience was hearing and the one in my head. I was telling myself I was going to die, and I wasn't even on skis. But then Judy Garland saved me.

My mother, who had a fascination for Judy Garland,

had always wanted to be an actress, and when I was growing up, she wanted me to be an actress, too. However, I was interested in more traditional learning, and when I received some college scholarships, Mom was upset. She would have much preferred that I head west to the Pasadena Playhouse to study acting.

As a child, I had seen Mom's disappointment when no talent scout came to our small Midwestern town and discovered either her considerable singing talent or her considerable beauty, and I felt both compassion and anger at her for being afraid to take the risks necessary to act on her dream. Nevertheless, her dream was not mine, and this created a climate of considerable tension between us. My dream was for an education. I loved to learn.

Now late into my sixth decade and with my odometer about to roll over into my seventh, I was allowing myself to own a part of me that had been too close to my mother's unrealistic fantasies for me to own earlier. It's true: I *love* to perform, I *love* an audience, and I *love it* when the energy in a room is high, things are moving quickly, and there is electricity in the air. Most of all I *love* the big stage, working under the lights, in the middle of the big top, and energizing as well as educating thousands of people to go forward to the lives they choose.

Well, this was the big stage, all right, and as Mom used to say (quoting Judy as the author), "The show must go on." I have no clue if Ms. Garland actually said these words, but I started repeating them, like a mantra, over and over in my head. The rhythm of these words, if not the meaning, calmed me down just enough so that I was able to do some rational thinking. *Teena,* I said to myself in my most stern voice, *just be yourself. If you pass out, you'll still have a good story to tell. If you want to, you can walk off the stage. Just be honest with your audience. After all, you are the first one to say how we can learn from our mistakes.* And it worked!

The more I gave myself permission to be me, the more I was aware that my body no longer perceived itself to be in danger. I reframed my anxiety by remembering a T-shirt I had given my girlfriend who experienced uncontrollable hot flashes. The shirt reframed her discomfort to that of a power surge, and now, I grabbed on to those words too. I gave a great performance, and after it was over, I realized that Mom had been mostly right about me. I do like to perform, but I don't like to act. Instead, I like to be. My type of entertainment is about being real.

A psychologist acquaintance recently called me an intellectual performance artist, and I love the term. Distanced from my youth and all of the traps I had seen Mom unable to avoid, I was finally able to embrace the part of me that came from her. The intellectual part comes from my love of learning, but the performance part comes from Mom. Mia, a terrific speaker in her own right (as are JC and Andy), recently came up to me after an energetic and electric presentation and said just one phrase: "Grandma Ellery lives." I knew immediately what she meant. The two of us embraced, both missing the woman with so much potential, born a generation too soon and without the supportive resources she needed to make her dreams come true, but with the resilience to offer resources to her own daughter, even though they might not have been what I wanted at the time.

Often the path of resilience leads us right back to where we began, to the strengths that were in us all along, and so I came to love doing keynotes (with or without advice from Judy Garland) as much as I do the smaller break-out sessions, and I continue to learn and to grow from my speaking experiences.

When speaking at large conventions, I am often on the ticket with famous actors, writers, or business leaders, and most of them have written a book. I decided that I needed to write a book, too. I looked at it as a tool, as something speakers do. And since I have worked with people for decades, it seemed natural that I would write what psychologists call a book on self-efficacy: a self-help book.

I made an outline and began to write. This is when I discovered that I hate self-help books. The practice of psychotherapy is both an art and a science, and the majority of these books often seem to be missing the art part. Don't get me wrong; the science part matters first, but truly great clinicians apply the science through their art.

This realization left me adrift, as I started and threw out many manuscripts over the next few months. In my writing, I tried to tell people how to live their lives, something I'm used to doing in my personal life four or five times a day, but in this context it felt false. I've never been shy about giving my opinion to family or friends, but I *know* my friends and family and they know me; they know my thoughts about them originate from my heart.

I come from the great Midwest and when I started speaking, I learned quickly that for me to have fun and feel authentic, I needed to speak as the sincere but light-hearted person that I am. After many false starts, I realized my success as a writer would depend on the same criteria: I needed to write from my heart. I am no good at making tools.

I also grew up idolizing as heroes the men and women who used both oratory and writing to drive social change in the nineteenth and twentieth centuries: Abraham Lincoln, Frederick Douglas, Elizabeth Cady Stanton, Susan B. Anthony, Florence Harding, Eleanor Roosevelt, Margaret Meade, Jane Addams, and many others.

From my earliest days I have seen myself as a writer. My very first writing prize was for an essay about my favorite childhood hero, Annie Oakley. (That's where I learned to use the lasso.) For several years I wrote a weekly newspaper column that combined psychological principles with family life. So I knew I could write, but I felt a little odd writing a book from the heart. After all, most people in my area of expertise write academic books, or scholarly books, or very good self-help books, even though I might not always read them. I was stuck. I could not *see* my book, I could not *feel* it, and I was about to abandon the whole idea.

Then, while preparing a talk for some very wise

women, I ran across a quote by the feminist theologian, Rosemary Radford Ruther. "It is through generating stories of our own crisis and hope, and telling them to one another, that we light the path." *That's what I am*, I thought. *I am a storyteller.* Throughout the ages women have connected through their stories. This is the heritage of my gender.

Instead of teaching about resilient living, I would *show* it by talking about my life and what I have learned. After all, Brooks had been trying to get me to write this book for ten years, but I had been too busy living it to write it. Could I teach what I have learned about resilience, leadership, courage, and love, by telling my story? Did I dare? If I wrote of my own life, what would people think? Would it be narcissistic? Would it be too revealing?

Professionals in the mental health field rarely write about their own lives. They write books based on research or theoretical models or clinical considerations. Well, maybe Freud wrote a lot from his life, but he was famous. I am neither famous nor a great academic. Would others disapprove if I wrote a book from my own experience? I pondered these thoughts for months, avoiding my computer as if it had the plague.

One hot July day I was babysitting my two-year-old granddaughter. We had taken a walk, it was not quite nap time, and when we returned we began to color. Ever the teacher, I decided we should practice drawing circles; one is never too young in Grandma's family to have a few pre-reading skills. I began to draw large, round circles and encouraged my granddaughter to do the same. But her circles were different than mine, and each was different from the other. Sometimes her circles had points like a star, sometimes they were more square, and sometimes they were lines that drifted off the page. She was making circles any way she wanted, circles that were unique to her. When I encouraged her, in my kindly but firm Grandma voice, to copy my circles, she turned to me with the natural assertiveness that only a two-year-old can muster and said, "No, Grandma. This is how *I* do circles."

I looked at this child, admired her spunkiness for taking on her determined grandma, and thought, *Who is the wise one here?* Her authenticity, combined with her high appraisal of her own potential, taught me more than I could ever teach her.

That's it, I thought. Life is really quite simple. You don't have to be older to be wise, you just have to know yourself. The trick is to embrace your personal strengths, all that you've learned so far, and everything that life has thrown at you: the good, the great, the bad, and the ugly. When you add determination and tenacity to this mixture, and you are willing to take some risks to drive your dreams forward, you can truly own who you are and have the best shot at a good life, no matter what. For me, I call this the Cahill factor: Teena Cahill using all she knows to be authentically Teena Cahill. For others it might be called the Donelli factor or the Klein factor or the Washington factor or the Dyer factor or the Gonzales factor or the Patel factor or the Wong factor. Every person on earth has a unique story, and the ability to turn adversity into advantage lives within each of us.

In that moment, sitting on the floor with my granddaughter on my lap, surrounded by crayons of many colors, my book appeared before my eyes. It would *not* be a tool; instead, it would be my story, from my heart, and handed down to other women as has been done for generations. *If I am lucky*, I thought, *these women will see my book as a small light on the path to resilient living. My path is different from theirs, as theirs is from mine, but the principles of turning adversity into advantage are constants that can draw us together to create a tight web of connectedness, and the tighter the web, the higher we bounce.*

My desire to learn may have started with the great orators of history, and the joy I feel when teaching may have come from my DNA, but the final permission to be who I am, both in print and on the big stage, was given to me by a tow-headed two-year-old with the last name Cahill.

Afterword

In the years since his injury, Brooks has made a remarkable cognitive recovery. Although he still experiences short-term memory loss and a general slowing down of his internal processing unit, he continues to surprise physicians and friends with his exceptional, ongoing progress. Despite his many challenges, he lives a full life. He meets daily for breakfast with a group of retired men who call themselves the Romeos. I didn't like the name of the group until I discovered it stands for Retired Old Men Eating Out. These fellows often follow breakfast with lunch and usually hit at least one university lecture a week. They take care of each other, support one another, and have formed a tight network of connectedness.

Brooks is in charge of the Veterans' Day Ceremony in our town, having built the event up from a small celebration to one where the police need to block off the road so they can accommodate the crowds that come to hear the bands play, the choirs sing, and the speakers speak. Brooks' involvement in organizing this event has reconnected him with his Marine buddies and helped him to forge a close relationship with the Marines at the nearby barracks. At the annual Marine Corps birthday luncheon he also helps to organize, he makes sure these active-duty Marines are the honored guests.

In spring or summer, Brooks can be seen sitting in his wheelchair in the backyard, coaching the grandkids to be great baseball, softball, football, and basketball players. He is vitally interested in their sports and is often the scorekeeper at their games. Sometimes he's the announcer, too.

Brooks is a strong, determined man, defined not by his limitations but by his strengths. Over the years, many aspects of his life have changed, but many others have not. He used his strength to direct his care when his life hung in the balance, and he has used it to build a new life once he was blessed with a second chance. Brooks has taught me many lessons, and his insistence on using his own strengths has made me stronger in my determination to use mine.

This understanding was made crystal clear to me a few years ago. We were in Scottsdale, Arizona, where I was the only presenter at a two-day event for executives. On these trips, I normally join the participants for lunch; then Brooks and I have dinner together. This time I was also invited to the evening events.

Brooks remains a pilot at heart and loves to travel. Although he is perfectly happy to spend a day or two in a hotel room watching CNN and getting to know the room service and housekeeping staff, I was feeling a little guilty about leaving him to eat dinner alone.

As I leaned over to kiss him goodbye, heading off yet again, he turned to me with his sweet smiling face, a room service table in front of him loaded with food, a glass of red wine in his hand, and his beloved St. Louis Cardinals on TV. "Dear, it doesn't get any better than this," he said.

I knew in that moment how richly my blessings flow.

•   •   •

As I finish this story, sitting in our not-quite-manicured backyard, surrounded by old, stately trees, my thoughts return to my childhood. It was the 1950s and my parents were part of the post-war migration to the suburbs. In our Ohio town of 30,000 residents, "the suburbs" meant a small ranch house, built at the edge of a cornfield.

I loved the stark beauty of that field, waves of green in the summer heat and paper-crisp stalks cut from their fruit and left to form rows of stubble when the snow fell. Even more, I loved the stand of trees at the far side of the field, remnants of a forgotten lot-line separating one farm from another. Sometimes I would walk through the field and stand beneath those trees—stalwart soldiers between corn and soybeans—just to feel their power. The first memory I have of yearning, of wanting something I didn't have, was for those magnificent trees. They were solid, powerful, and grounded symbols of where I wanted to live, of how I wanted my life to feel.

I have learned since that what I was yearning for at the edge of that long-ago cornfield were not the trees themselves, but rather the feelings of contentment and growth reflected by the power, majesty, and harmony that surrounded me when I stood in their presence.

Today, I know that we don't need to look for a stand of trees in the distance, already grown, outside of ourselves, to generate those feelings in our lives. We can raise our own saplings—a whole forest if we want to—by planting seeds, tending them carefully, and if we are lucky, watching them grow into the future we choose.

I have lived in a time and place surrounded by that opportunity to grow, and because of this I consider myself one of the most fortunate people to have ever walked the earth. My seeds, planted decades ago in the rich Ohio soil, have sprouted and flourished, and their power lives deep within me.

"We shall not cease from exploration.
And the end of all our exploring
Will be to arrive where we started and
know the place for the first time."
T. S. Eliot

Bibliography

Barber and Walson, 2002, *Listen Up*, St. Martin's Griffin Press, NYC.

Beck, A. T., Rush, A. J., Shaw, B. F., Emery, G., 1979, *The Cognitive Theory of Depression*, Guilford Press.

Eliot, John 2004, *Overachievement: The New Model for Exceptional Performance*, Penguin Books, NY.

Gilligan, C., 1982, *In a Different Voice: Psychological Theory and Women's Development*, Harvard University Press, Cambridge, MA.

Goleman, Daniel, 1996, *Emotional Intelligence*, Bantam Books, NY.

Groopman, Jerome, 2004, *The Anatomy of Hope*, Random House, NY.

Moss-Kantor, Rosabeth, 2006, *Confidence: How Winning Streaks and Losing Streaks Begin and End*, Crown Business Publishing, NY.

Seligman, Martin, 1990, *Learned Optimism: How to Change Your Mind and Your Life,* Free Press, NY.

Vaillant, G. E., 2002, *Aging Well,* Little, Brown, Boston.

Seligman, Martin, 2002, *Authentic Happiness: Using the New Positive Psychology to Realize Your Potential for Lasting Fulfillment,* Free Press, NY

Sharma, Robin, 1999, *The Monk Who Sold His Ferrari: A fable about fulfilling your dreams and reaching your destiny,* Hay House, Inc.

Organizational Resources

American Psychological Association
750 First Street NE
Washington DC 20002
www.apa.org

American Stroke Association
National Center
7272 Greenville Avenue
Dallas TX 75231
www.strokeassociation.org

Family Caregiver Alliance
180 Montgomery Street
San Francisco, CA 94104
www.caregiver.org

National Family Caregivers Association
10400 Connecticut Avenue, Suite 500
Kensington, MD 20895-3944
www.nfcacares.org

National Spinal Cord Injury Association
6701 Democracy Blvd.
Suite 300-9.
Bethesda, MD 20817
www.spinalcord.org